SO YOUR CHI...
A DO...

SO YOUR CHILDREN WANT A DOG?

Katie Patmore

Consultant: John Rogerson

POPULAR DOGS
London Sydney Auckland Johannesburg

To my dearest Husband;
and Thomas
and Matthew.
With all my love.
Thank you for your patience.

Popular Dogs Publishing Co. Ltd

An imprint of the Random Century Group
20 Vauxhall Bridge Road, London SW1V 2SA

Random Century Australia (Pty) Ltd
20 Alfred Street, Milsons Point, Sydney 2061

Random Century New Zealand Limited
PO Box 40–086, Glenfield, Auckland 10

Century Hutchinson South Africa (Pty) Ltd
PO Box 337, Bergvlei 2012, South Africa

First published 1991

Set in Sabon and Optima by
Speedset Ltd, Ellesmere Port, South Wirral
Printed and bound in Great Britain
by Mackays of Chatham PLC, Chatham, Kent

A catalogue record for this book is available upon
request from the British Library

ISBN 0 09 174927 1

Contents

Acknowledgements

THERE are many people without whose help this book would never have been written.

My special thanks to Muriel and Frank Ekman, who had enough confidence in me to ask if I would teach dog training at their club. I would never have started otherwise and I shall be eternally grateful.

John Rogerson has taught me more than anyone else about dog behaviour. His profound knowledge, coupled with his willingness to pass this on to myself and others, has enabled me, not only to set up a Behaviour Clinic, but also to contemplate writing a book in the first place. His patient understanding and support in the writing of this book have been invaluable and I am deeply grateful.

I would like to thank sincerely Derek Greaves for taking the excellent photographs. Photographing children is not easy; neither is it easy to photograph dogs. Trying to photograph the two together is twice as difficult. His patience and good humour throughout was really appreciated. Also, thank you to all owners, their children and their dogs for enabling Derek to take these splendid photographs.

Veterinary surgeons are extremely busy people; therefore, 'thank you' hardly seems sufficient for David Newton BA, BVSc, MRCVS for all the time taken in reading the manuscript and discussing it with me. His advice has been of immense value.

Roy Hunter kindly gave his comments and advice from over 30 years' experience of dogs. I would like to express my gratitude to him. Thanks also to Rosemary Chambers who obtained her first puppy as I was writing the book and gave very helpful comments.

This book was written in longhand and Kath Hardman deserves special thanks for having the unenviable task of deciphering my dreadful handwriting.

My brother, Nicolas Soames urged me to write this book. His

support and encouragement never wavered and I am truly grateful to him. I wish also to thank all the owners and their dogs for the experience and knowledge they have given me.

And lastly Nimrod, for making my introduction to dog ownership such a joy. He is truly a wonderful companion and I thank him so much for that.

Foreword

IT is no mere coincidence that with the explosion in the pet dog population, the number of animal charities being asked to take in dogs that are no longer wanted by their owners is also increasing dramatically. Why would an owner want to part with the family pet you may ask yourself. Well a survey recently carried out by one of the leading animal welfare organizations lists behavioural problems as one of the most common reasons that dogs are given up for adoption. And just why do these behavioural problems develop? The answer is sometimes because of inappropriate breed selection in the first place, or more commonly because of a complete failure to understand the dog's requirements. Lots of pet dog owners base their knowledge of bringing up a puppy on handed down half truths, myths and old wives tales.

Our children are the next generation of dog owners and where are they going to learn how to select, care for and train their dogs? How can they learn to be responsible pet owners when there are often adults in their community who fail to understand their pets or their responsibilities towards them.

If our children are to grow up as responsible dog owners we must finally lay to rest the old school of 'if he messes rub his nose in it' with the more acceptable form of upbringing based on an understanding of our companion animals. Katie Patmore is one of the 'new wave' of trainers who, besides having an understanding of the mechanics of how to train a dog also has a deep rooted interest in understanding how to interpret and modify behaviour. This in itself is extremely significant because dog training and behaviour are linked and, for the most part, are inseparable. If we now add Katie's knowledge of children into the list of ingredients required for the production of this book, we end up with a recipe that should ensure that our future dog owners maintain the status of their companions as 'best friends' rather than as liabilities.

Leo Bustad, the Dean of Washington State Veterinary School once said, 'Our survival as a species depends on our ability to foster a boundless compassion for living things.' The timeless bond that exists between ourselves and our dogs that continues to play such an important role in family life has to be based on a mutual understanding. It is by learning to understand our dogs that we may perhaps be able to learn to understand ourselves a little better.

John Rogerson

CHAPTER · 1

Mummy, Can We Have a Dog?

I HAD not intended to get another dog. We already had two (a 13-year-old placid male crossbred and a very bouncy 9-year-old Springer Spaniel bitch).

I took the children to see some 4-day-old puppies. That was mistake number one. They looked like sausages on sticks and were doing nothing but feeding and sleeping; but the children were mesmerized. We visited again a week later. The puppies were crawling about the box a little more and nuzzling into the children's hands. Fatal. On the third visit the puppies were much more active, playing with one another and of course, coming to greet any visitors with great joy. It was after this visit, on the way home in the car, that I was asked 'Mummy, can we have another dog?' That was how Wally came to join our family.

Easy isn't it?

However, there are many things to consider first. It is essential to think hard particularly before buying your first dog. Most adults and children love puppies. They are appealing, adorable, cuddly, relatively easy to control and the larger breeds are still small at this age. But, not all people, or children for that matter, feel the same once the puppies become adolescent or even adult dogs; and they do not remain puppies for very long. However, they are very dependent animals and your family will remain responsible for him for the rest of his life, which could be up to about 16 years.

Companionship

Your dog will require human companionship for a large part of each day; even more while he is young. Puppies get lonely and up to mischief if left to their own devices for more than an hour or two.

Dogs are pack animals. That means that they instinctively prefer to live in social groups. Although our dogs have been selectively bred and domesticated, in many respects they are not too dissimilar from the wolf from whom they are descended. Even the Poodle which could not look less like a wolf, still has some of the same basic instincts and one of these is to live within a pack or social group. This group can be made up of other canines or, as we generally mean when talking about dogs today, a human family or pack. From the puppy's point of view, when he comes to your home, he is merely transferring from one pack comprising the dam or mother and littermates to another, your family.

Dogs need to get used to being on their own for part of the day, but it is unfair for dogs to be left on their own all day and every day during the week while their owners are at work and school.

Do you have this sort of time? Will you have this sort of time next year, the year after that and the years after that?

Many people feel that one way out of this problem is to get two dogs, littermates perhaps (or even one dog each for your two children!). The puppies will be company for each other, you say. Well, look at it another way. Not only are there two puppies to get up to mischief and two puppies to housetrain, but, two puppies constantly together become a canine pack within a human pack. They will not need to relate to you as they have all they need from each other. They will be each other's best friend, playing and having fun more with each other than with you. In a human pack that does not bode very well. They will be less keen to please you and therefore they will be difficult to train.

Play is very important to puppies and dogs; that is how they learn to relate to other dogs (and people) and if it comes mainly from other dogs, *that is who they will relate to.*

Training

The dog will also relate to the person who trains him better than he relates to the person who feeds him. Will you have the time and patience to do this? If a child undertakes this task, is he old enough? Eleven to twelve years of age is a rough guide and his ability to train a dog successfully depends upon the breed and size of dog.

Has your child enough time and energy after school? Just training at the weekends and during holidays is not enough. In fact, training a dog does not just involve teaching him to walk to heel and sit, training also means preventing anti-social behaviour, such as barking at the gasman, as well as the more positive aspects of teaching him his name and to come for example. This is carried on during your puppy's waking moments. Your child spends most of his day at school.

Will your child be able to manage the puppy when he is fully grown?

To live acceptably in human society, a dog needs to learn to associate a minimum of eight words: his name, come, no, sit, down, stay, heel and most important 'good boy'. He is not born with these in his head, I'm afraid. A dog learns by association and these words have to be taught to him by patient repetition and immediate reward. *Everyone in the family needs to have the same attitude to his training otherwise he will become confused.*

Training a dog is simple, but, requires time and patience and is better done by the owner. Although some people do send their dogs away to be trained, you may lose out on the special relationship you will form with a dog you have trained yourself. You may also miss learning to understand your dog and what makes him tick, and all the rewards that that brings. Dogs are not machines that you can programme for the rest of their lives. They are living animals and prey to many influences acting upon them. Occasionally throughout their lives, an incident or change in situation may necessitate part of this training to be reinforced. If you have not originally trained him yourself, you will not know how to do this.

The other important reason for not sending your dog away to be trained is that training actually starts when you get him home, not several months later when a trainer will accept him and by then, without training, you may all be very discouraged by his anti-social behaviour.

Training and Babies

If you have a baby on the way, or a tiny baby already in existence, the common feeling is that it will be marvellous for them (the dog and child) to grow up together. This sounds lovely, I agree; but could you cope with nappies and housetraining, or a child you are trying to potty train and cleaning up accidents from a child and dog? Or a child who naturally spends most of his time on the floor, amongst the dog hairs, sharing his toys and biscuits with a slobbery dog? (See photograph 1). Bouncy dogs can knock children over; when children are learning to walk, they are not too steady. How fair is it on them to be knocked over? How fair is it on the dog to be poked and pulled and fallen upon by very young children who know no better? It might be a lot fairer on both to wait until the child is at least of an age to start nursery school.

Expense

'It can come out of my pocket money and I will go without sweets for the next two months.' Do not be fooled. The amount of pocket money children get varies enormously, but, apart from perhaps being able to afford a feeding and water bowl and the odd new collar and lead or a toy at Christmas, that is it. The rest – the major expenses – are up to you.

Putting aside the expense of actually obtaining the dog which may be from nothing to as much as £1000 or more for a rare breed, there will be many other expenses during the dog's life.

Equipment

To start with he will need a bed of some sort, although a cardboard box will be adequate for a month or two, depending on the size of dog. If you are going to crate train him (see page 36) you will need to buy a crate, although it is sometimes possible to find a pet shop from whom you can hire one. He will also need grooming equipment, collars and leads and a feeding and water bowl.

Health

The first major expense will be vaccinations. The dog will require a course of injections starting at about eight weeks, before he can safely be taken where other dogs go; he will then require a booster injection once a year *for the rest of his life.* He will also need to be wormed regularly and he may require a vaccination against kennel cough, which can be repeated once or twice each year (see page 42). To prevent unwanted litters of puppies you may want to have your bitch neutered (spayed). Many male dogs make more congenial and biddable pets if they are also neutered (castrated).

None of this is free. There is no National Health Service for dogs that become ill or have an accident. There are charities which help if you are on a very low income or there are insurance schemes which can be obtained if you are not. However, neither charities nor insurance schemes cover vaccinations or neutering. They are for accidents and illnesses only and treatment is paid for at the time. Although some breeds may have a pre-disposition to certain medical conditions all dogs can become ill, from the best pedigree to the scruffiest mutt.

Feeding
Feeding is probably the next major expense. This of course depends upon what you feed your dog and the size of him. Obviously, it costs more to feed a St Bernard than a Yorkshire Terrier and a very active dog will eat more than a dog that spends most of his day in front of the fire.

Holidays
If you go abroad regularly for your holidays, plans will have to be made for your dog. You do not generally take dogs abroad for a two week holiday as he will have to spend six months in quarantine kennels on return to protect against bringing rabies into Great Britain.

For holidays in this country, it is surprising how many hotels, self-catering cottages and campsites will accept well behaved dogs. This obviously cuts down the cost of having your dog looked after. However, if it is necessary to leave him, kennel fees will add to the cost of the holiday; and last minute holidays without the dog may be impossible in the high season when many good kennels may already be booked up.

Grooming
Some breeds – Terriers and Poodles for example – need to be stripped (hair plucked out) and clipped (hair cut using clippers) regularly. For Poodles it may be as often as every six weeks. Long-haired breeds that have been allowed to slip into a tangled mess may require help from a professional groomer.

Cars

Surprisingly little thought is given to this aspect of owning a dog. Large dogs and small children do not travel well when squeezed together, albeit strapped in the back of a saloon car; arms get squashed and tempers frayed. Estate or hatchback cars are undoubtedly better for transporting medium to large canines and humans of various sizes, the dog being safely ensconced at the back behind a grille. A very small dog, however, can sit happily in a harness on the back seat, providing you do not have too many children.

Gardens

Your garden will never be the same again! A bitch's urine marks the lawn, unless you are prepared to follow her with a bucket of water to wash away the urine; and shrubs wilt at the sight of a cocked leg. However, your garden is the area for your dog to use. From there you will clean up what the dog deposits and it will not offend anyone.

Dogs will run all over the garden. A flower bed is as much there to be romped upon as a lawn, from the dog's point of view. However, it is possible to train dogs to keep off the flower beds. As with any other aspect of the dog's life, this requires time and patience. The garden should be fenced to keep the dog from straying on to roads. It is extremely unwise to try and train a dog to keep to an unfenced garden in an urban environment or country area surrounded by sheep and cattle. *Dogs are animals and can forget their training in one second at the sight of a running cat or quick whiff of sheep.*

House

Dogs are not for the excessively houseproud. They inevitably bring in extra dust and general dirt. Dog hairs get left on carpets, around soft furnishings and on a clean school uniform. You will inevitably get housetraining accidents with a young puppy and while there is absolutely no need for destructiveness to be excessive, some minor acts do occur in most puppy-owning households.

Exercise

How much exercise does a dog need? There are considerable variations of a dog's requirements, depending on size, age and breed. It does not necessarily follow that a small dog needs less exercise than a big one. A Terrier for example, has far more bouncy energy than some Great

Danes, and working breeds are more energetic. However, even for a Great Dane, a boring walk to the shops and back is not sufficient. Generally, dogs require one or two exercise sessions a day. Exercise means being allowed to run free in an area safe from cars and grazing animals, where the dog can enjoy himself without being a nuisance to anyone. If your child undertakes to be responsible for this aspect of the dog's welfare, is he sturdy enough for a dog that may grow big and strong in a few months? Is he sensible enough to control even a small dog?

Trying to combine walking the dog with a paper-round is not exercise to a dog and is the same to him as the boring walk to the shops and back. It can also be fraught with the difficulties of coping with strays, dogs let out to wander alone and dogs minding their own business in their own gardens. They might be quite happy with a paper-boy, but not with his four-legged companion.

If you have children who are of the age when they go to playgrounds, it can seem sensible to combine the two activities of exercising the dog and keeping the children happy. However, dogs should not be taken to a children's play area, frightening children and perhaps knocking them down, however well intentioned the dog is. Many playgrounds do not allow dogs because of fouling of these areas.

As exercise is required each day, if it is raining all week you will get wet! A pushchair with a completely waterproof cover is essential for the baby!

So Why Get a Dog at All?

If you are prepared for all these points, owning a dog can give you one of the greatest pleasures in life.

Companionship

A dog, to a large extent, is what you make him, but he has the capacity to become your best friend; a true companion who accepts you, whatever your mood, warts and all. He can give you trust and affection with no strings attached.

Feelings of loneliness rapidly diminish when you own a dog. When you go out for a walk with him, you are far more likely to make a new acquaintance than if on your own. Dog owners tend to stop and talk to each other, either about dogs generally or simply to admire each other's dogs; this tends to make you feel proud and raises your self esteem. There is a growing body of medical opinion which feels that contact with dogs can actually lower blood pressure and help sick people recover more quickly.

'Her even cheerful temperament can be relied upon (unlike others in the house). She often cheers me up.' A father talking about his first dog.

Training

Training a dog can and should be good fun. It is simple and need not be very time consuming, although patience, a sense of humour and a consistent attitude towards the dog are all vital ingredients. Joining a good training club (see page 80) will help with the basics and more if you want; you will make friends as well. However, training starts when the dog comes to your house and because dogs are simple creatures compared to their human owners, this can become a rewarding and satisfying activity in a world surrounded by complications.

Expense, Gardens, House

The cost of keeping a dog and the inconvenience he can cause generally, can only be measured against the delight he brings to you and your family. To my mind, the pleasure a dog brings to one's life as a whole, far outweighs any inconvenience or the financial cost expended upon him.

Dogs and Children

Although children have to be taught and helped to play the right games with dogs, and dogs have to be taught that they are subordinate to children, dogs and children who have passed the pre-school age can make wonderful companions.

Children quickly learn the art of patience, essential when owning a dog. They learn to care for and consider a dependent living being other than themselves. (Owning a pet dog can introduce children to the facts of life.) Older children can be taught how to teach the dog simple exercises which can be fun for the dog and children alike. (See photograph 3). For children who are shy or lacking in confidence, this can give them a sense of achievement and therefore a changed attitude towards life in general.

Parents can be grumpy and cross after a bad day, but the dog still wags his tail and shows unreserved affection.

'I didn't expect her to enjoy playing football. If nobody else will play with me, Daisy will.' Six-year-old boy talking about his family's first dog.

CHAPTER · 2

Choosing a Dog with Children in Mind

WHEN I chose my first dog, I was not married and I didn't have any children. I was living on my own, with a cat, in a new town with a new job and feeling lonely. A colleague suggested getting a dog. At first, I thought it was an extraordinary idea. They may as well have suggested an elephant! A litter of crossbred dogs became available, the result of an accident in the park. I knew nothing about dogs, but, fortunately, I seemed to pick the right one for me. He turned out to be better than I could ever have hoped; he was bigger – a lot bigger, than I thought he was going to be, but he accepted everything that came his way – my marriage, children and more dogs, without so much as an 'excuse me, I was here first!'. I was lucky. It was mainly luck. There was no conscious thought on my part to choose the right dog for me. But I only had myself and my cat to consider; no children running all over the place with the odd poking finger. The choice of my subsequent dogs was given much more thorough consideration, although the amount of exercise my second dog, a Springer Spaniel, required was not taken into account. She was fully able to bounce to the ceiling and back even after a long walk. My husband found the constant activity trying and I became fit!

There are 7.3 million dogs in Britain and they were all adorable puppies at the beginning of their lives. Unfortunately, not all of these 7.3 million dogs have grown into pleasant acceptable pets. Rescue homes are usually bursting with dogs which have been rejected for one reason or another and vets' notice boards and pet columns in newspapers are full of 'free to good home' puppies and adolescent dogs or older dogs with a tag of 'genuine reason for sale'. Many of these dogs were probably chosen with the best of intentions, but some of these choices could possibly have been made with more informed thought. Only you can make the choice. It is personal; but it is possible for you to be helped to make the right choice for you.

Pedigree or Mongrel

The choice between pedigree or mongrel is usually the first decision to be made. Do you give a mongrel you feel sorry for a home in case it is put down if no one wants it, or do you get a pedigree dog? Usually, a pedigree will cost a great deal more to buy, but, the cost of keeping either is the same. A pedigree will grow into the likeness of its breed; you will be able to be sure of its eventual size, shape and colour. It is possible to predict what kind of coat he will eventually have – long or short, curly or straight, wiry or silky. Temperament (see page 13), which is the most important factor when choosing a dog, particularly with children in mind, is not quite so predictable, but far more so than with a non-pedigree dog. You will have a general idea whether he will be inclined to be more friendly than aloof, for example.

On the other hand, a true mongrel, a real Heinz 57, is an unknown quantity. His ancestry is unclear. He may be totally different from both his parents, if they are known at all, in temperament, size and coat type. There are many mongrels which are wonderful with children around; kind, patient and tolerant. However, in a family new to the ins and outs of dog ownership and with very young children, it can be rather a gamble. Waiting until the children are older would be more appropriate if you want a mongrel for a first dog. If deciding upon a mongrel a puppy may prove to be less of a risk.

Crossbreeds

Crossbred dogs are dogs of mixed parentage, when one or both parents or ancestors are from a recognized breed. These dogs may often be described as a first or second cross. Sometimes such a cross is purposefully produced in order that good characteristics of the dam (mother) or sire (father) are produced in the puppies. If the best characteristics do come out in the puppies, you can get an excellent dog, however, the reverse can just as easily be true.

Working Dogs

There are many advertisements these days, for dogs from working parents, particularly Border Collies: 'Farm bred Border Collies, working parents. Can be seen. Ideal pets.' These appear regularly in newspapers.

Those dogs may have lovely temperaments, be just the right size and colour for you with the sort of coat you like. But, they are working dogs. They are bred to work. They need to work. If they are not worked, they can make poor pets. Watch the television programme *One Man and His*

Dog. Would you be able to give one of these dogs the exercise and stimulation he requires to satisfy his instincts? He will not be the only demand on your time with children around. He needs to run and herd. That is what he was bred to do. Denied this basic requirement, he can become neurotic and his chasing urges will find anti-social outlets, such as cars, children, bicycles, joggers or other dogs. Of course, there are lovely Border Collies that live successfully in families, but the exercise and stimulative play that these dogs are given are not easily available in most families with children.

There are other breeds, particularly Labradors, Retrievers, Flat-coated Retrievers, Springer Spaniels and German Shepherd Dogs some of which have been bred to work; and although the temperament of some may be felt to be ideal for children, the more working 'stock' the dog has in its ancestry, the more its instincts will be to the fore and the more those instincts will require satisfying in order to produce a relatively satisfied and well adjusted pet. However, these dogs often possess sound and biddable temperaments.

Show Dogs
These days it seems there are two types of many of the working breeds. You can get a working Labrador and a show Labrador; a working Springer Spaniel and a show Springer Spaniel. Similarly with Border Collies. The 'show' dog of working breeds tends to be larger and broader than the actual working dog. This particularly applies to Labradors and Springers. The other difference is in their need to work. Some show Border Collies have never seen a sheep; and because they have been selectively bred over several generations, the working stock in their genes has been weakened and the need to work to satisfy their instincts is weaker. Therefore, they will make an easier dog to have with children around.

Adult or Puppy

Shall we go to the dogs' home and give a poor unwanted adult dog a loving home, or shall we start with a puppy?

Adult dogs are readily available in almost any breed you could wish for, including crossbreeds or mongrels. It may appear to you that grown dogs will come already trained and so will be easier to manage. No whining at night for the company of its littermates; no housetraining problems; no chewing; no pulling on the lead. The advantages can seem endless. But ask yourself another question. Why is this dog for sale?

Some grown dogs are available because of a change in home

circumstances. Both owners may need to work for an unforeseen reason. They may have had a baby who is allergic to that particular dog's hair; happily not a common situation, but it happens; owners do divorce, die, or leave the country. These are some of what I would call 'genuine reason for sale' and you may get a happy, healthy and well-balanced dog. But many of the dogs requiring new homes do so due to lack of training or perhaps lack of general care. They may have developed really ingrained habits of chewing, barking, wandering or even aggression. They may be nervous or over-sensitive or not very tolerant of children. They may never have been properly housetrained. These dogs may simply have been the wrong sort of dog for those particular people, but in their eagerness to get rid of the dog, some people may not be totally honest about the anti-social habits that have been allowed to develop. These dogs may be hard to rehabilitate, especially if they have been passed from one home to another.

Breeding or show kennels sometimes have dogs which are surplus to their requirements, or have not developed physically how the owner would have liked; for example, ears not quite correct or coat markings not quite true. This may not matter to you or I, but if these dogs are over 16 weeks and have been kept in a kennel with their mother or other dogs with little access to human, everyday life, they may be difficult to housetrain, but, more importantly, they will be very difficult to socialize if they have had little human contact. How would that dog react to your young children and their friends coming to call?

You need to be prepared to put a considerable amount of time and effort into re-training an older puppy or an adult dog. This can be a rewarding challenge, but you must be prepared for it. For a family with young children, who have never had a dog before, I would not advise it unless you are very certain of the background of the dog you are taking on. It is generally better to buy a puppy rather than an older dog when young children are around. He will then fit more readily into your lifestyle and you will really get to know and understand your dog from early in his life.

Dog or Bitch

This is a question everyone must face when selecting a pet. In general, the bitch tends to be more biddable, affectionate and loyal than the male dog. They are usually more gentle with children and more devoted as a companion.

The bitch will come into season ('heat' or 'oestrum') when she is between 8 and 12 months old and, thereafter, at 6 to 10 month intervals, continuing for the rest of her life unless she is spayed (a surgical operation completely removing her reproductive organs). When in season, which lasts for about 21 days, she will have to be kept apart from male dogs. She may be generally more excitable and may try to escape because she will have the urge to mate.

The male dog, particularly of the larger and/or more dominant breeds and dogs from the Terrier group of dogs (see page 16) tend to be more independent, outward looking and require firmer handling than the bitch. They are usually more headstrong and may be inclined to escape and wander away from home. Castration (surgical removal of the testicles) may, with some re-training, help some of these problems.

Although many male dogs do adapt very well to the lifestyle within your family and can be gentle and tolerant of children, for the family with no experience of owning a dog, the best choice is generally a bitch.

Temperament

This is the most important factor when choosing dogs with children in mind. Dogs chosen for families where there are children require very careful thought. Temperament is more important than size, colour or type of coat. These dogs need to be patient and tolerant. They require a placid, well-adjusted even temperament. They should be neither too bold or dominant, nor too shy and sensitive. They should take sudden noises easily in their stride and accept visitors, whether they are your friends' children, their parents or babysitters.

Think of yourselves as well. What type of family are you? Are you bouncy and perhaps a bit bossy? Then a slightly more bold dog requiring firmer handling may fit better into your family; but families that lead a more calm and quiet existence (difficult with children, but it does happen) may find a slightly sensitive dog would suit their needs more satisfactorily.

The dog also has to be chosen with the person in mind who will spend most time with him. Dad may be able to manage a big, bold and bouncy animal at weekends when he walks the dog on his own; but could mum manage a dog like that with a baby in a pushchair and a toddler hanging on?

Exercise

You need to ask yourself some questions on this subject. How much exercise do you normally take? This must be walking exercise because you can't exercise a dog while you are on your exercise bicycle, nor can you take the dog to the swimming pool! Do you take no exercise at the moment? Some when the sun is out and it is warm and dry? Or do you walk regularly and enjoy it in most weathers? The majority of families fall somewhere in between the second and third categories. All dogs require regular exercise each day, regardless of the weather; but some dogs need more than most, some of the Terriers particularly.

Many of the Gundog breeds, for example Retrievers, Labradors and Setters, are often considered when choosing a dog with children in mind, because of their tolerant temperament; but like Terriers and some of the larger breeds, such as German Shepherds, they have a high exercise requirement. If the amount of exercise you are able to give a dog is more of an issue to you than the size of the dog, then a Cavalier King Charles Spaniel, for example, is an excellent pet with children and will be content with a more moderate amount of exercise.

Coat

There is a great and beautiful variety in the types of coat dogs have, ranging from the Old English Sheepdog (Dulux dog) and the Shih Tzu to the smooth coated Boxer and the Italian Greyhound. There is even the Mexican Hairless Dog. However, every dog's coat needs attention, but some more than others, and all dogs need to be groomed daily (see page 59).

The Dulux dog which you see on television and the long-haired breeds you see winning at Crufts, parading with their glorious coats, not a hair out of place, have had hours of effort put in to making their coats so immaculate. With perhaps a couple of children and all that that entails, will you have the time and energy left to keep the dog's coat free of tangles, let alone anything more? You need to be prepared for that. If you like long coats, generally the more silky the texture, the easier it is to keep to an acceptable standard. Yorkshire Terriers, Bernese Mountain Dogs, Cockers, Springers, Retrievers and the Setters, to name but a few, all have silky coats. There are some variations however; the Rough Collie (Lassie dog) has an abundant coat not particularly silky, but it is actually relatively easy to keep looking attractive. Remember though, that in wet weather, the fuller the coat, the greater the amount of water that will be brought into your house. One shake before being rubbed down and the children have developed brown measles and the walls will have a stunning new pattern! Short-coated dogs, although needing to be regularly groomed, are generally less work; but, remember even the short-coated dogs can leave hairs all over the place. That Dalmatian's beautiful coat will shed! A stray hair from his coat is just as likely to end up in the scrambled egg as one from a long-coated dog.

Terriers and Poodles have different coats again. The coats of most Terrier breeds tend to be thick, harsh and more wiry. Generally, they are hand stripped about two to three times a year, otherwise ordinary regular grooming keeps the coat in good condition. Poodles require clipping every six weeks. It is possible to clip the dog with a pair of scissors, but many people find the task tedious and go to a dog grooming parlour. Because these dogs lose their hair in this way, Poodles are usually a good choice for families where asthma or an allergy to dog hair is a problem.

Size

Dogs can vary in size from the tiny Chihuahua weighing about 3 lbs to the majestic Irish Wolfhound, weighing about 140 lbs. However, size is not necessarily an indication of the amount of space required. Great Danes and Irish Wolfhounds are very large dogs, but are usually calm and can curl up in a relatively small corner. On the other hand, Setters for example, particularly the Irish Red Setter and the bouncy Labrador tend to be lively and exuberant and can sweep your child's orange juice to the floor in one easy wag of the tail. Lively, exuberant dogs require more space than calm, sedate ones, regardless of size. The excitable Bearded Collie can be like a friendly bull in a china shop. Children can be as much barged past to see who is at the door, as can the Lego house they may have just built.

One point to remember: very small dogs require a lot of bending down to, not very good if you have a bad back, and some dogs become very strong. If a grandparent, for example, is to be enlisted to look after the dog from time to time, could he or she manage your adult pet?

Choosing the Right Breed with Children in Mind

If you have decided on a pedigree, it can be confusing when it comes to choosing the right one for you as there are about 200 breeds of dog. Dogs are divided by the Kennel Club into six groups.

The Gundog Group includes Retrievers, Labradors, Spaniels and Setters; most gundogs tend to be excellent with children, kind, patient and tolerant. They are usually energetic (Springers are not called Springers for nothing!) but are generally very accepting of the comings and goings of visitors.

This acceptance of visitors is not so, I'm afraid, with some of the dogs from the Working Group. These include the German Shepherd Dogs, Dobermanns, Rottweilers and St Bernards. The dogs from this group are usually very good with the children of their family, but some, particularly those from guarding breeds, can be suspicious of strangers. If you lead a busy social life, with babysitters coming and going with some regularity, then these dogs may not be an ideal choice.

Generally, the breeds in the Hound Group are hunters and include dogs as different as the Beagle and the Saluki. Most of those from this group tend to be rather aloof and have strong instincts to hunt by either sight or scent which can cause them to wander; one whiff of something exciting for example, and they are off! Therefore, they can be difficult to keep as pets in families who want a nice leisurely walk collecting acorns and conkers in the woods.

The Terrier Group includes dogs as large as the Airedale and as small as the Norfolk Terrier. Most of the Terriers tend to be rough, tough dogs and are not averse to a scrap. Although they are inclined to be rather outward looking, particularly the males of this group, they are alert dogs and full of fun and character, while retaining a stubbornness that some people find frustrating. They are very energetic dogs!

Dogs from the Toy Group are often thought of as lap dogs and are much less energetic than the Terriers, but are tougher than people generally think. They vary in temperament, from the sensitive and affectionate Italian Greyhound to the more aloof, less patient Pekinese.

All the dogs which do not seem to fit into any of the other groups are in the Utility Group. They include dogs as different as the courageous Bulldog to the lively Dalmatian and the intelligent Shih Tzu.

Libraries and book shops have some excellent books on breeds which will give you some idea of size, temperament and good and not such good points of the various breeds. But be aware of what some descriptions really mean. It can be rather like an estate agent's description of a house which they want to sell. You need to decipher the descriptions. For example, a dog may be described as good with children but also as loyal and an excellent guard/house dog. This means that it will be good with the children of the family, but possibly not so accepting of visiting children and their parents. Tireless is another term used. Sounds fun, but are you tireless? Visiting a dog show might help to give you some idea of sizes and coats and so on, but do bear in mind that each individual breeder will feel that their own breed is best and may not be entirely impartial!

The Right Time to Buy

Age of Children

Dogs grow and develop very much more quickly than children, so the often heard saying that 'we want the dog and child to grow up together' does not really ring true.

Some dogs can have extremely bouncy puppyhoods, Retrievers for example, so a baby that is learning to walk can become frustrated and upset if constantly knocked down. Children around 2 years old are apt to tease dogs and little fingers are not averse to giving the odd poke. They need to be taught not to, but children can take a while to learn and in the meantime, the dog is not forming a favourable opinion of the children he is supposed to love. It is true that many families with young babies who acquire a puppy do cope well and with much enjoyment, but given a choice, the best age is around the time the child might start nursery school and any time after that. In that way, you have a bit of time for teaching the dog how to live in your family (the pack he belongs to) and the dog has a break from perhaps an over-attentive child, and your child is able to build a car out of bricks on the floor without them being knocked over! When at home, the child is gradually becoming sensible enough to be helped to play some simple games with the dog, under your supervision (see page 52).

Time of Year

The best time for buying puppies is undoubtedly spring. The weather is getting warmer, so going outside in order to train your dog to be clean in the house, is more pleasant, even in the dark, than when it is freezing cold and possibly wet as well. The back door is more likely to be open and this encourages your dog to use the garden more often than the living room carpet.

Once the dog has finished his vaccinations and is allowed where other dogs go, you are more likely to take him with you, for example to school and back, when the weather is pleasant (human nature being what it is!) rather than you just bundling him into the back of the car and going to the park and back without having met many people. Families naturally spend more time going out and about in summer than winter; and he will become better socialized, an essential ingredient if you want a well adjusted dog who accepts and enjoys his role in life.

Summer holidays will need to be carefully planned. Occasionally, breeders will accept puppies back, but he will be fine in good kennels when he is around 6 months of age and onwards. Or you could take him with you if you are able to.

By the time the hectic Christmas season arrives, your dog will have adapted to the lifestyle of your family and will most likely be settled and sensible enough to allow the children to open their presents without feeling the need to chew each new toy as it appears or making straight for the Christmas tree decorations! (See photograph 2).

If you have friends who have dogs, visit them and see for yourself what a particular type of dog is like in an ordinary home, remembering that all dogs are different and how they are brought up affects their behaviour. Talk to people who see a variety of dogs: veterinary surgeons, dog trainers, one of the growing number of dog behaviourists; also dog groomers and the owners of boarding kennels.

Listen to all and inform yourself, but, ultimately, the final decision must belong to your family alone. There are many dogs to choose from and somewhere there is the right one for your circumstances; one which will fit well into your family and remain with you all his life.

CHAPTER · 3

Choosing the Right Puppy for a Family with Children

WHEN I was asked by my children if we could have another dog, I have to say that nothing was further from my mind. I had certainly never intended to get a Cavalier King Charles Spaniel, nor had I intended to get an English Springer Spaniel 9 years ago. I had not actually gone out and looked for a dog, or even thought particularly hard about what sort of dog I might have. I knew, when the situation presented itself, that these pups were the right ones for us at that particular time and at that stage of our lives.

There are four common elements in the background of all our dogs. I knew the mother of each of them. They were all bought from the place where they were actually born. They were all born in home surroundings and kept there, rather than put in a kennel, away from the house, until we took them home with us, and, most importantly, they had all been regularly handled by children before they joined our family.

Where to Buy a Puppy

It is extremely easy to buy a puppy. Too easy. But to know where to buy the right puppy is often more difficult than it seems. I get many calls asking me where a puppy of a particular breed can be obtained. Mongrel and crossbred puppies can be bought from rescue organizations, private homes (casual breeders) and still, unfortunately, some pet shops. Pedigree puppies can be bought from the same places and also from professional breeders and puppy farms.

Puppy Farms
Puppies are not born on a puppy farm. They are obtained from people who may be miles away from the 'farm' and there is usually a very large selection of breeds available for sale, 25 not being uncommon, usually

of the most popular ones. You will have no idea of what his first weeks of life were like. Nor will you have any idea of the temperament of his mother, because she will be with the person who bred from her.

Animal Welfare Organizations

These also contain puppies whose history is unknown. Perhaps they have been dumped, the result of unplanned, unwanted litters. They may have been taken there by their owners who were unable to find homes for them. Sometimes a bitch is taken in with her still suckling puppies. I have seen some bitches like this, which bark furiously at every approach by people. What does this tell the puppies about people? (See page 21, The Right Mother). This is not how puppies should learn to react to the humans they are going to live with for the rest of their lives.

Pet Shops

It used to be possible to buy a puppy from almost every pet shop. 'How much is that doggy in the window' did not arise from imagination. This encouraged prospective dog owners to buy on impulse with insufficient thought given to the whole business of owning a dog. Fortunately, now there are far fewer pet shops selling puppies. Puppies are very impressionable. What opinion is he forming of life when he may have been teased through the window with possibly a bang on it first to attract his attention. Is it too hot or draughty? Who was his mum? How carefully has he been handled?

Casual Breeders

Casual breeders are people who have never bred a litter before, or perhaps breed the occasional litter, but do not do it professionally. They may have purposefully bred from their bitch. These planned matings can produce some lovely puppies. It is often because of the temperament of the dam that these people have wanted to breed from her, and they have usually gone to a lot of time and effort to find a suitable sire. The whole mating and whelping will have been carefully overseen and although experience may be lacking, this is usually amply made up for in the care given and concern to 'do the best'. This can apply to the first and second crosses, bearing in mind that if the best characteristics of the dam and sire come out in the puppies, you may get an excellent dog. But the reverse can also be true.

Also in this category can come 'accidents'. The bitch got out whilst in season and has mated with an ardent male who was left wandering around looking for just such an opportunity! Although you will not know who sired the puppies, if the dam is of good temperament and you do not want a full pedigree dog, one from a litter such as this will be less of a risk than one where both parents are unknown. However, ask the breeder why she has bred from her. If she has bred to improve the behaviour of her bitch, then you need to consider that she may have produced a litter of puppies with the same problem behaviour.

Professional Breeders

These people usually specialize in one or two breeds. They have knowledge of their breeds although they may be a little biased! They will usually be experienced in the whole business of mating and whelping and most will care well for the dam, feeding her well and not breeding from her too often. Unfortunately, however, a few do not take such care and are more concerned with the money they might make. You must obtain, from the breeder, the Kennel Club registration papers when you purchase your puppy. This will ensure that the bitch has not had more than one litter per year or five in her lifetime. This helps to ensure the quality of her puppies. Some professional breeders may breed for colour, size or other physical attributes. *Temperament is by far the most important and should be the prime consideration.*

The Right Mother

The Dam

Genetically speaking the puppies tend to reflect their parents' qualities and defects, particularly those of the mother. The puppies' future behaviour patterns will be most like hers. She is particularly important and you must see her with the puppies. Behind a grille in a kennel, or on her own is not good enough. Not only is it she who teaches the puppies to accept discipline, but it is she who indicates to the puppies what people are like. If she barks and growls and generally displays anti-social behaviour when you visit the puppies, this is what the puppies will learn. They will detect fear and unfriendliness in her and associate that with people. This mistrust will increase as the puppies grow older. Nervous bitches tend to produce nervous puppies.

When you visit, the mother should allow you near the puppies; she should be happy for you to pick them up, cradle them in your arms, play with them and generally give them attention. She should accept this attention given to her puppies, by all of you, parents and children.

Children

Are there children in the family of the breeder? If not, have the puppies had contact with children? Have children handled them? Puppies can be squirming, wriggly little bundles. To prevent inexperienced little fingers inadvertently digging in when picking a puppy up, it is often better at first for an adult to pick the puppy up and give him to a child who is already seated. (See photograph 4). Puppies are very playful in the last few weeks before going to their new homes. Puppies that have had contact with children then, tend to settle quicker and are more accepting of them than puppies that have not had this sort of contact.

Life Surrounding the Puppies

Ideally the puppies will be in the house in which they were born, rather than in a kennel in the garden. Puppies are very impressionable and learn more in the first few weeks of their lives than is generally supposed. Your puppy is to live in a family with children and all the hustle and bustle that surrounds them.

When your puppy joins your household, life does not stop. The children might wish it would but it doesn't. They bang the front door when they come home from school; their bags are dropped unceremoniously on the hall floor, and babies cry; the telephone rings; the hoover will come out occasionally and the washing machine is constantly on the go. If your puppy has lived his last impressionable weeks before coming to you in a kennel at the bottom of the garden, all this is going to come as a shock to him and he may find it difficult to adjust. Puppies that have been born and kept in a house, albeit a relatively quiet corner perhaps, are far more likely to take these everyday unavoidable happenings in their stride. There is no need for breeders to bombard their puppies purposefully with extraordinary noises and situations. The ordinary disorder around everyday life will do the job adequately.

An aspect which might not be covered by everyday life with the breeder is car travel. However, most dogs these days have to get used to travelling frequently in cars. This is part of normal life. It is less harrowing for the puppy if he has his first journey with his mother and littermates and perhaps some journeys when only one or two puppies go together.

Cleanliness

Dogs instinctively like to keep their sleeping area clean. This is one of the reasons they are able to live in our houses. It is important that the puppies' sleeping area is kept clean, otherwise they will become used to living and sleeping in filth. This may make housetraining difficult later on.

How would you cope with a dog, hairs and all, sharing the floor with your child?

Below: Training should be fun and it can be an absorbing hobby

2. Having a young inquisitive puppy at Christmas necessitates a half decorated tree or chewed decorations, not to mention toys! Apart from causing frayed tempers, it can be a danger to the puppy

4. This mother is quite happy for the children to handle and play with her puppies. The children are on the floor so that there is no danger of the puppies being accidentally dropped

5. The sofa is not for this puppy: she is learning from the start where her place is to be. She will not have to experience a change in later life that she will not understand

6. She is also getting to know where her place is in the car

7. Just putting the puppy outside and leaving him to get on with relieving himself will not teach him what he is out there for. He will probably come in and do it on the carpet

8. These two young puppies know their food is there but are learning to wait patiently until their pack leader has finished her meal

9. Crate training gives a dog a break from an overattentive child and aids housetraining and chewing problems. This dog is happily settled in his den

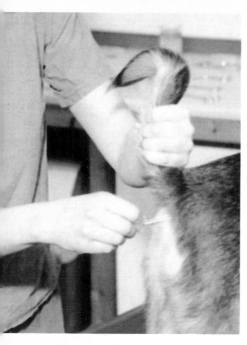
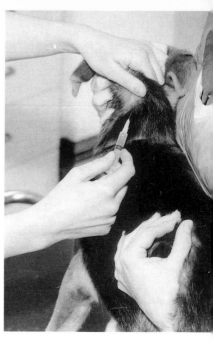

10. This 16-week-old puppy is having her temperature taken before being given her final vaccination

11. She is just about to be given her injection

12. Kennel cough vaccine is being dripped into this dog's nose. Dogs that are used to being handled from a young age are very much easier to treat

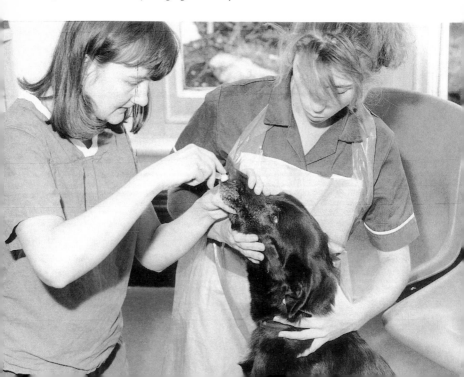

Choosing a Puppy from a Litter

Your puppy is going to live with you for about 10 possibly 15 years. He will be part of your family through all the ups and downs that everyday life throws upon you. Therefore choosing the right puppy to fit in with your life is not something you should do on just one visit. You need to make two or three visits or more if you can. You want to observe the puppies eating as well as playing. They may be very sleepy on one visit, especially if they have just eaten. Choosing the right puppy from a sleeping furry mass is difficult! They all look cuddly.

You should choose the puppy yourself. Do not accept that the breeder just brings out one puppy for you to look at, saying that you could have that one. You should choose the one you want. Of course listen to what they say regarding the behaviour of any particular puppy; after all they are the people who have spent most time watching and observing them and they will know them best. But you need to see the different puppies yourself.

All puppies from a litter tend to appear very similar indeed, particularly on the first visit. They are all lively little bundles of fun which seem to be roughly the same size, colour and shape. They all appear friendly and playful to a greater or lesser degree. So how do you choose?

Puppies even in the same litter will all have slightly different characteristics. These characteristics will become more marked as the puppies grow older. This is not too dissimilar to babies. Look what different adults we grow into!

Dogs are pack animals. In a pack there is a leader and there are followers. A litter of puppies is a pack and within this little canine pack, leaders and followers are already evident, even at 5 weeks of age which is when people usually make their first visit. There will be one puppy which is the most dominant and there will be one puppy which will be the most submissive. Taking the most dominant as No. 1 and the most submissive as No. 5 in a litter of five puppies for example, let us look at the behaviour of each of these puppies.

The Dominant Puppy

The dominant puppy, the No. 1, may well be the largest as he (or she, as it is not always a male which is the most dominant) will make absolutely sure he is first to the food and has as much as he wants. He will not be pushed out by another puppy trying to get part of what he considers to be his. He will usually initiate a lot of play with the other puppies and if they are playing with a toy, he will be the one to get it and keep it for himself. It will be he who will greet you first and he will appear unreservedly friendly. He will probably be described as the 'boisterous one' or the 'trouble maker' or the one that is 'into everything', having been first to explore new areas away from the whelping box. This puppy often appears full of character, fun and mischief. Travel on in time, a few months. How much fun will these characteristics be in a fully grown dog? His mother will keep him firmly in place. Could you? A dominant puppy requires dominant handling. That doesn't mean constantly hitting him with a rolled up newspaper. It means having a generally bossy, no-nonsense attitude towards him. You can love him and you can play with him, but you must be a strong boss otherwise he will end up as leader in your pack. Training this sort of puppy can be very difficult and frustrating. It means having this attitude from the start. Now. Even though he is so small and appealing. You must think of the children. He must be subordinate to them too; and that is going to be even more difficult than it may be for you. If you are choosing a large breed and your children are young, he will grow bigger than they are in a few short months and his pushy 'here I am folks' attitude is not going to make for a very harmonious life within your family. However, even a small breed of dog can make life difficult as he assumes the role of leader.

It is this puppy that is often described by owners as having 'chosen' them, having been the first to greet them. However, this bold little puppy will choose anyone! *Unless you are experienced, leave this puppy*; he will be the right one for someone else such as a trainer or someone very experienced with dogs.

The Submissive Puppy
Now let us look at No. 5 puppy, the most submissive one. He will be almost the exact opposite of his 'into everything' littermate. He will be pushed out of the feeding bowl; he will be rarely, if at all, the one to initiate play and he will lose all battles over a toy. This puppy, if he is not nervous or too cowering may be fine in a quiet, organized home with few comings and goings; but it would be unfair to expect him to cope with the hustle and bustle of ordinary family life, let alone the chaotic life that some families lead. Do not be tempted to take this poor little thing home with you, although he is sitting in a corner and looking sad and lonely. Well adjusted relationships are not founded on pity!

The One To Choose
The puppy to choose is somewhere between No. 1 and No. 5. He should be friendly but not too pushy, and he should be bright and alert to what

A well adjusted puppy will allow himself to be picked up and cuddled without struggling like this one is

is going on around him. He should play happily with his littermates, but also be happy to come and play with you. He should have more of an 'excuse me, here I am' attitude than the more overpowering No. 1.

Pick up the puppies, one at a time and cradle them in your arms. Does he settle without too much of a struggle? Or does he struggle and perhaps try to nip your fingers? A well adjusted puppy will tolerate picking up and general handling without displaying protesting aggression (too dominant) or undue panic (too nervous). Look also at the temperament of the dam. Is she bossy, pushy or perhaps over-friendly? Or does she roll on her back when you bend down to stroke her? Some breeds tend to be more dominant, Giant Schnauzers for example, and some breeds are naturally more submissive, Shetland Sheepdogs for example. If the dam is quite dominant, then choose a puppy that is low down in the hierarchy, perhaps No. 4. If the reverse is true and she is very submissive, then a pup nearer the top of the hierarchy, perhaps No. 2 would make a good pet.

You Have Chosen Your Puppy – What Next?

Age to Bring Home
The best age to bring your puppy home is around 6 to 8 weeks. When

the puppy is between 3 to 12 weeks old, he goes through what is called the socialization period. It is during this period that he is forming his attitudes to the world around him.

Bringing a puppy home earlier than 6 weeks may cause him to be less responsive to discipline; his mother, from whom he learns, has not had sufficient time to teach him. It is during this socialization period that he learns about being a dog; about playing (and fighting) and about what various body postures mean. He cannot learn that from us and he will not learn it later. Not learning it may cause him to misunderstand other dogs. This can lead to nervousness in the company of dogs, and aggression.

Puppies over 16 weeks, sometimes even 14 weeks, that have been kept in a kennel with other dogs may be impossible to socialize adequately with humans. Their attitude to life is formed and if this has not included regular and close contact with people, they will grow into dogs that are more orientated towards dogs than to humans. Since our pet dogs live in a human society, a dog like this has a very poor start and it may never be possible to make up for it. It could also be difficult to housetrain these dogs and it might be impossible to achieve any form of reliability.

Bedding

Think ahead to the first night. Your puppy will miss not only the warmth of his littermates but also their smell. Smell is very important to dogs, and yours, however pleasant, will be unfamiliar to him. Either take an old blanket or buy a furry 'basket' and ask the breeder to leave it in the room where the puppies are, for a few days prior to your taking the puppy home. Ask them not to wash it, unless there has been an accident. The puppies should be allowed unlimited access to this bed and when you take it home with your puppy, there will be something familiar for him to snuggle into. A hot water bottle, put in his basket (stone if you have one) will help that first night.

If you are going to crate train your dog (see page 36), one will need to be bought. Remember that your puppy will rattle around in it at first, but you need to buy one large enough for when he is older as he will grow at an alarming rate.

Sleeping Arrangements

Decide on this now.

Your dog is a pack animal. The leader sleeps in the safest, warmest, most comfortable area. You are the leader and the bedroom is your den. *The puppy is subordinate and you should decide where he sleeps.* It is not cruel for him to sleep on his own downstairs, in the kitchen, perhaps. He is a dog, not a human. The first night, and possibly the second and third, he will cry (see page 32) but he will not come to any psychological harm at all! Start as you mean to go on.

Diet Sheet
A few days before you pick the puppy up, ask the breeder for a diet sheet. You want information such as time of feeds, quantities and of course what the puppy is actually being fed on, as you will need to keep to the same food for a week or two, or more if it is what you want your puppy to be fed on. Drastic, sudden changes in diet can upset his tummy.

Equipment
You will need a feeding bowl, although some breeders may give you what the puppy has been using. Not essential, but a nice touch. You will also need to buy a water bowl, a soft light-weight collar (nylon or canvas is best for the first one) and a similarly light lead. He will need to be groomed; a soft brush is best to start with.

Housetraining
Keep all your old newspapers and buy a bottle of liquid especially made to clean the area and remove the smell – usually obtainable from vets, or some pet shops. (See page 35).

Toys
The children may like to buy these. It can even come out of their pocket money! Do not be tempted to allow the children to give one of their toys to the puppy, however altruistic that may seem! Your puppy will not be able to tell the difference between the toys they allow him to play with and toys they do not. This includes shoes and slippers. A new one is much the same to your puppy as an old one. In any case, the children will have to keep their toys as tidy as possible for quite a while.

Gates and Gardens
Make sure that the puppy cannot get out of the garden, or at least has an area where he is safe. It is a good idea to start training the children to keep the gate closed. Children's habits die hard and puppies are very quick!

What Shall We Call Him?
Your puppy is a dog, a canine. He is not a little furry human on four

speedy legs. So give him a dog's name. Calling him George (or Susan if you are going to have a bitch) only encourages owners (and friends) to think of him as a furry human. There are certain 'human' names which have now become established dog names, such as Ben or Sophie, but why not let your imagination go and make up an unusual name? Keep it short, one or two syllables and try to think ahead to the vocabulary you will be using to train him (see page 3) and make his name different from these words. 'Kit' is too close to 'Sit' for example. Children are good at making up names; they are not yet bound by the constraints we now have. You should all agree to keep to that name, and not change it from say, Cass to Cassie.

Veterinary Surgeon

Finally, you will need to find a vet. Either ask the breeder who they use, if they are local to you, or ask friends who have dogs. Personal recommendation is best. Failing that, Yellow Pages or your library will have a list. You will need to be able to get to your veterinary surgeon quite easily, but he doesn't have to be just round the corner.

Then relax. For the first few weeks after your puppy comes home with you, life will be hectic.

Exciting and fun, but hectic!

CHAPTER · 4

The Puppy's First 24 Hours with You and Your Children

WE picked up Wally rather late on a Saturday afternoon during the last week in February. He was the tiniest, fluffiest bundle with a beautiful face. We also collected the bed we had left with the breeder, put him in the back of the car, put him in it and drove home. The children leaned over the back seat and stroked him. He was probably bewildered and certainly quiet for the whole of the short journey.

When we arrived home, I carried him into the garden. He had a very tentative sniff around and very fortunately did a wee after about 15 minutes. A long time but well worth the wait. I thought that was a very good start and told him so.

We took him in the house and allowed him to explore in his own time. There was only one small area that was out of bounds to him, (behind the television where there are many wires) and I just said 'Aaah!' in a short guttural voice as he approached it and he moved quickly away. The children watched him all the time, fascinated. They picked him up too much but he was very cuddly . . .!

I gave him a tiny meal (hardly a mouthful by comparison to my other dogs) of which he only ate half and I took him outside. He didn't do anything, he just sat down. I brought him in, put him in his basket and let him sleep. When he awoke, we were all in another room so he did a wee in the kitchen (my fault for not keeping an eye on him) and came to find us. The children sat on the floor and cuddled and played with him until it was time for them to go to bed, which they reluctantly did after a hundred 'good nights' to Wally.

When the time came for us to go to bed, I was thankful it wasn't raining, because I had to wait outside for half an hour before he relieved himself. And so to bed, in the kitchen, in his basket, in the crate (door of crate open), newspaper on the floor, light off, door closed. And I was lucky. Not a peep out of him until 6 a.m. when he started barking.

The children were already awake and longing to go in. However, I had no intention of being woken each morning by a squeak and therefore I banged loudly on the kitchen door and sent the children back up. Ten minutes later, Wally was still quiet, so we all went in and got a really friendly 'good morning' welcome. This made all the extra work and lack of sleep, due to the early start, worth every minute.

Start as You Mean to Go On

This is the most important rule to follow with any dog that comes to your family. Dogs thrive contentedly in situations where they know their place. Their place is at the bottom of the pack.

When he comes to your family he doesn't think 'I'm a dog and you are human'; we are all animals in his eyes. As far as he is concerned he has exchanged one pack (his littermates) for another (your family). He is a pack animal and must have a leader. If one is not forthcoming, then he will (gradually and subtly perhaps) assume that role for himself. So be a leader from the start.

A leader, from the dog's point of view – and that is what you must realize, from the dog's point of view, not yours – has certain privileges. The leader of a pack puts himself first. He sleeps in the most comfortable area (see Sleeping Arrangements, page 26), he eats first (see Feeding, page 37) and he decides on the rules of games (see Games, page 52). He also decides whether he wants to play or not. The dog is subordinate and should decide none of these things. He will understand that. He is a dog and must be subordinate to all the family members.

Being a leader does *not* mean stomping around or shouting or hitting him with a rolled up newspaper. This should never be done to a puppy. It will make him fearful, not subordinate. Your puppy will also need to know what he can and cannot do; where he can and cannot go. If for example you do not want him upstairs when he is older, larger or hairier, or when your baby arrives (see page 87), he doesn't go upstairs today, tomorrow or ever. Not even when he has a bath and you are in a soft mood. He will not feel it is unfair. He is not human. As far as he is concerned, he is not allowed upstairs and that is that. He may try to come up several times, but if he meets with the same reaction each time, he will learn very quickly. This also applies to where his place is when travelling in the car and whether he is allowed on the furniture. (See photograph 5).

The only barrier to what might otherwise be a simple life, with your dog knowing his place and being aware of exactly what he can and cannot do, are your feelings of guilt (perhaps) of him lying at your feet rather than on your lap, for example. Of course, it is lovely to have a dog curling up on your knees all soft and warm. If you want him on your lap as an adult dog fine (see page 97, Who is the Boss?) but if not, put him on the floor from the beginning. Now.

Prevention is much easier than cure. Dogs do not think like us. They do not reason or ask why and will readily accept a fair, consistent attitude to the rules that must surround our lives. They will be happier and more content and will repay your efforts to provide this consistency by being a joy to have around.

Fetching Your Puppy from the Breeder

The day has arrived and everyone will be excited. You are all prepared. Choose a day which is free of interruptions and one when you will have the time to devote to making the adjustment which will occur to your family lifestyle, as easy as possible, always remembering that the puppy adjusts his life around yours. Inevitably, you will have to make some changes to your life, such as allowing extra time to devote to housetraining in the first few weeks. *But your life should not be ruled by your dog.*

The time to pick him up is largely up to you and the breeder, but late morning to early afternoon is best to give the puppy time to settle. Take a towel for him to sit on and something warm to cover him with if it is cold and you have a long journey. Put him in the car where you will want him to be on future journeys. Talk to him soothingly and he can be stroked (not by the driver!), but keep him where his place is to be. Not on the children's laps! Take him straight home. Friends or relatives might kindly ask you to call in on the way home so they can see the puppy, but there will be time for all that when he has adjusted to his new pack. Get him home and settled. In any case, he must not go where other dogs have been until he is fully protected by vaccinations (see page 41).

Arrival at Home

Let the puppy explore the garden first. The reasons for this are obvious. This is where you want him to go to urinate and defecate; and the chances are that after his journey, he will want to do just that. Put him down and allow him to wander (the garden should be securely fenced). Discourage the children from distracting him. When he has relieved himself, give him lots of praise and bring him in. Allow him to explore there too, but only where he is allowed of course. Start as you mean to go on.

Once he has had a good wander and perhaps a little play, take him out again. He may then want to sleep. Puppies sleep a lot and must be allowed to do so. Explain to the children that he is very young and requires a lot of sleep to help him grow well and contentedly. Take him outside again when he awakes. Then he may require a meal. Prepare your meal with his (coffee and a biscuit will do if it is not your mealtime) and when you have eaten yours (pack leader eats first) give him his. He probably won't eat all of his first few meals as he may be a bit unsettled, so take the food up after 10 minutes, taking him into the garden again after he has eaten. Explain to the children that puppies need to go a lot and must be trained to use the garden rather then the house. Puppies do not learn this automatically.

This kind of activity continues until bedtime.

The First Night
The moment most new puppy owners dread.

Take him out and wait until he has relieved himself, put him in his bed with the blanket you brought from the breeder and a ticking clock, a stone hot water bottle or a rubber one well wrapped to keep him warm and help induce sleep, newspaper on the floor and go to bed yourself. Ignore any whining or crying. This is hard but essential. If you take him up to bed with you, that is where he will want to be each night. The bedroom is your den – not his. If you go in to him and give him a cuddle to comfort him and settle him down, that, as far as he is concerned is a wonderful reward for his crying and that behaviour will be perpetuated. *Ignore if possible*, but if you must go down, make a really loud noise on the door. That way the door is horrible to him each time he squeaks, not you. It will not spoil his relationship with you and he will learn very quickly that his crying does not bring pleasure. So he will eventually stop. Be patient and consistent. It is no good going in to give him a cuddle several times one night and then, when you and the children are tired and grumpy through lack of sleep, present to him a different attitude. He will not understand the change in approach and will become confused and more persistent.

The First Morning
The rule is that no one is to go into him unless he is quiet. He is not to learn that whining is to bring you in to him. A quick, loud bang on the door, about 5 minutes of quiet and in you go, greeting him calmly. Do not tell him off for having messed on the paper or elsewhere. Just clear it up. Take him out. Again, stay with him until he has done something. Lots of praise and then bring him in.

The children will of course be down and if they are old enough and sensible enough, let them play with the puppy or keep an eye on him while you prepare your and the puppy's breakfast. Eat yours, then give the puppy his. Again, he might not eat it all. Leave it down for 10 minutes then throw away whatever is remaining.

If you have to take the children to school, you have to take them to school and that is that. Similarly, if you have to do some shopping. Leave your puppy where he slept at night, newspaper on the floor. Be quite matter of fact, no over affectionate goodbyes. Be back as quickly as possible. This is the first time you are leaving him. He will have to get used to being left, but make it short to start with. Again, do not return to him without listening to hear if he is quiet before you return. The same rule applies for being on his own during the day, as for the first night. In his eyes it must be his quietness that is bringing you back, not his whining. Again greet him calmly and enjoy his company.

In these first 24 hours, your puppy's life has begun to acquire some of the shape it will continue to have throughout his life. He is beginning to learn what is expected of him. There are certain important elements he has already learnt about his new world.

Dogs, Children and Travel

The children will all want to cuddle the puppy on their laps. But think ahead: how would a large dog, straight from the woods, happy, but very wet and muddy be accepted on a lap? Not very well. Dogs are creatures of habit. They are not mini humans in a fur coat. They are dogs; however tiny your puppy is, he is still a dog. If you intend him to travel on the back seat, then that is where he goes; if you intend him to travel in the back of an estate car behind a grille, then that is where he goes – right from the start. Not tomorrow, or next week, or simply when he is bigger (how much bigger?). He will accept it, no questions asked, because he knows no different. (See photograph 6).

He should not be allowed to travel in a car with his head hanging out of the window; other vehicles passing too close, present a danger. He should not be allowed to jump out of the car until you have attached the lead. This can be extremely dangerous. However, on his first journey, it is unlikely that he will try, but as he becomes more confident, he may become excited at the prospect of getting out of the car. Even a tiny puppy can be trained to get out only on command. Open the door slightly and if he rushes forward say in a commanding voice 'Back' or 'Wait' and push him back with your hand. Close the door again and repeat until he is waiting for you to allow him to get out. Lots of praise, of course, when he does wait. If you travel frequently by bus or train, he needs to get used to this as soon as possible. Again, start as you mean to go on. He travels where you want him to travel when he is an adult dog, bearing in mind that on public transport, dogs are not allowed on the seats.

Housetraining

Your puppy will not housetrain himself. He requires your watchful eye to help him learn that your house is not his lavatory. Housetraining needs vigilance; the more vigilant you are during the first few weeks, the quicker your puppy will learn where he can relieve himself.

You will require a great deal of patience and you need to remember the following:

1. Before he is 12 weeks old, he is not able to control his bodily functions for very long. Therefore he will need to be taken out after meals, drink, play and sleep – even a 10 minute nap.
2. He will want to move away from his bed before relieving himself.
3. Once your puppy is clean and dry at night, he will still need to go more frequently during the day. Eating, drinking and playing stimulates his need to eliminate. During the night his body is at rest.
4. Your puppy will not ask to go out until he is virtually completely reliable in the house. Some puppies never ask to go out if the owner has been vigilant and lets them out frequently. These puppies/dogs know they will eventually be let out and will wait.
5. When there are children in the family, accidents most frequently occur when they are busily playing or otherwise occupied. When they come out of school and you are preparing supper, no one really watches the puppy properly; either bring him in the kitchen with you so that you are watching him, or if you are crate training him (see page 36), put him in the crate, door closed for that half hour or so. *Prevention is easier than cure.*

If you are really watchful of your puppy, you will begin to learn the warning signs he gives before he goes; usually a puppy will sniff to find a good spot and then he may circle if he wants to defecate. He will certainly need to go after sleeping and playing; and about 5 minutes after eating and drinking. He may also need to go at other times if about an hour has elapsed since he last did something.

Rules

The rules for housetraining are as follows:

1. Take your puppy out and stay with him. Do not put him outside and close the door. He will have no idea what he is out there for. (See photograph 7).

2. As he is actually relieving himself use a word such as 'Hurry up', 'Be quick' or any word you will feel happy about using in front of other people. 'Do a poo' might not be one of them! He will gradually learn to associate the word with what he is doing and will eventually relieve himself on command.
3. Give lots of praise once he has done what you took him out to do.
4. Discourage the children from distracting him from the job in hand. If your children are sensible enough, take them out with you the first few times, so that they can learn what to do and the command you use, stressing to them that this command must be used in a consistent tone of voice as the puppy is actually eliminating. Satisfy yourself that they know what they are doing. In this way the whole family can take part in this more onerous aspect of bringing up a puppy.
5. If your puppy has an accident in the house, you can *only* tell him off if you catch him in the act. Then say a sharp 'No' or 'Aaah' (in a guttural voice) and quickly take him out to a spot where he normally goes. If you caught him quickly enough, he may still want to do some more. If not, and 10 minutes later you are still there, take him back in and watch him.

    If you do not catch him in the act, you cannot tell him off. He will not connect the telling off with what he has produced on your carpet and he will become confused. It is cruel to rub his nose in it. *Under no circumstances should this ever be done.* It may even encourage him to eat his faeces.
6. Clean up any accident with a liquid specially made for this purpose, obtainable from vets or pet shops. Some ammonia based cleansers can smell like stale urine and may encourage dogs to go to the same spot again. Some of these cleansers may cause severe irritation to the skin or respiratory system.
7. Use newspaper at night and when you are out. Make sure he goes on there by covering a relatively large area to start with and gradually reducing it. Place the paper as far from the bed as possible to encourage the pup to keep his sleeping area clean. Once he is about 16 weeks old and he is clean most nights, take up the newspaper. It may only be encouraging him to keep using it.
8. Accidents during the day are largely the fault of the owners' lack of vigilance. There are bound to be some accidents, life does go on; the children do get engrossed in things other than watching the puppy. But, remember, the more watchful you are during the first few weeks, the quicker your puppy will be at using the garden more than the carpet. There will be times when you cannot watch him; either

confine him with a fireguard around his basket, as most dogs will not mess their sleeping area, or crate train him.

Crate Training

Crate training greatly reduces the chance of accidents. It works on the principle that dogs that have been born and kept in clean conditions, and most have, are reluctant to mess their sleeping quarters.

It means that when you cannot watch the puppy, or when the children are playing wildly in the garden and getting the puppy over excited (see page 55, Rough and Tumble), he can be put somewhere he cannot get up to mischief or learn bad habits. The puppy can also have a break from an overattentive child. Chewing problems are minimized and you can all have an occasional break from keeping an eye on him. (See photograph 9). However much you love your puppy and however keen the children are to watch him, there will not only be times when you cannot watch him but also times when you want a break.

If you have a young baby who is crawling and learning to walk, crate training your puppy can make the difference between enjoying both these living creatures or tearing your hair out!

The rules for crate training are as follows:

1. The crate will need to be large enough for him to sit, stand, lie down and turn around. When he is a puppy he will require quite a small crate; but he will grow quickly and require another one in a few months. To save the expense of buying another one (they are not cheap), either hire one or buy one which will be big enough for the grown dog, remembering that some breeds, Labradors particularly, can be unreliable in their chewing habits up to a year old or more. For the puppy this may be large enough for him to relieve himself at one end of the crate and then lie down at the other end. This is not the object of the exercise! If your puppy does this, do not tell him off. Just block off one end with either a sheet of thick perspex or rigid wire mesh. Whichever you use, it must be securely fastened top, bottom and sides, with no bits hanging loose. Puppies are very inquisitive.
2. Put his basket in there and that is where he sleeps or goes when you want him out of mischief's way. He will regard it as a 'den'. Some puppies settle more quickly if you cover the crate, just leaving the front open, thus making it cosy and warm.
3. Shake the crate a little. Some are very 'rattley' and the pup needs to get used to the noise.

4. He should *always* associate going in the crate with something pleasurable, taking the form of praise or praise and a titbit. Give him a command such as 'Basket' or 'Bed' or other of your choosing (but be consistent) and encourage him in with titbits or a toy. Also let him go in and out at will.

5. *Never send him to the crate as punishment.*

6. After a few days, when he is happily going in there and he appears sleepy, close the door of the crate. If he goes to sleep, leave him, door closed, but listen or keep an eye on him. When he awakes, before he squeaks, let him out. Again, his squeaking must not be what is letting him out. If he just lies there, potter about, talking to him from time to time and let him out after 2 to 3 minutes, or certainly while he is still happy.

7. And so you continue, gradually leaving him for longer periods, occasionally going out of the house and leaving him in his crate. Remember that very young puppies cannot 'hold on' for too long. So if you are going to be out for 1 to 2 hours, make sure he relieves himself before you go. Do not close it at night yet.

8. From about 12 to 14 weeks onwards, you will start to have nights when he is clean and dry. Therefore, from around 15 to 16 weeks of age you can close the crate at night.

9. If he does mess in there, do not tell him off. Just thoroughly clean it up and make a mental note that you either left him in there too long or he didn't relieve himself before he went in.

10. Some puppies wee a little in excitement at your homecoming. This is unintentional and it does not mean he has soiled his sleeping area. He is not aware of doing it and should not be told off. This phase will pass, just greet him and let him out very calmly indeed! Thoroughly clean his bed.

11. Never let him out of the crate when he is barking. Wait until he is quiet.

12. He should never regard the crate as 'his'. You should be able to get him out whenever *you* want to. You should be able to stroke him in there whenever *you* want to. So should the children. With puppies, the best way to do this is with titbits, so that hands going into his crate always mean something pleasant.

Feeding

During these first 24 hours, your puppy has also learnt that he is not important enough to be fed first. (See photograph 8).

Praise

Most puppies actually want to please their leader, believe it or not.

Praise must be given when the puppy is doing what you want him to do, or at least within 1 or 2 seconds. For example, when he has relieved himself in the garden, the praise must come then and there, not once you have gone back in the house; he will have forgotten all about it.

No or Aaah!

Your puppy has to learn this quickly. The problem is that in a household with young children, 'No' is a very overworked word. Unfortunately, this is a fact of life! For the puppy, therefore, an 'Aaah!' growled from the back of your throat is much more effective. This should be voiced just as your puppy is starting to do what he shouldn't, not when he has finished. For instance, if you see he is about to pick up something he shouldn't, a quick 'Aaah!' is more effective than telling him off after he has done it and is already wandering over to his bed to have a good chew. The sound should be harsh enough to make the puppy stop in his tracks.

You have now given your puppy a good idea of what his life will be like with all of you. There will be no sudden or dramatic changes to his lifestyle as he grows older (and bigger) and he will develop securely and contentedly in the knowledge that your *attitude is consistent*.

CHAPTER · 5

Health

ONE problem I have never had is any difficulty in getting an immediate response when I call my dogs back to me. They have always come instantly and happily. The difficulty with Daisy, my English Springer Spaniel, crept up on me rather insidiously, mainly because she never went very far away and if she did go further, she was back before I needed to call her. Inevitably, however, there were times when I had to call her. The first time she did not come back was, of course, when there were a number of people in the woods, most of whom knew me. Daisy was not very far away, sniffing at something she evidently found absorbing; I called her quite normally and received no response. I was surprised and the people around started to take an interest when on my third call, she was still sniffing – some of these people had had recall problems with their dogs and had come to me for help. Their dogs were now fine; but there was I, supposedly knowing what to do, with a dog which took no notice whatsoever of my voice. We all had a good laugh, I went to get her and wondered why this had suddenly happened to an 8-year-old dog.

It never occurred to me that she could have hearing problems, although she is a Spaniel with ears that are far too long and heavy. Also, she had not been scratching them any more than usual. This problem continued to a greater or lesser degree for a few weeks. The time I realized that she may have a physical as opposed to a training problem was when I came home one day and she was not there to greet me as she always is. She was not asleep; I could hear her walking around upstairs. I called her and got no response. A visit to the veterinary surgeon was clearly necessary. Daisy was thoroughly examined and her ears were found to be full of wax around the drums; although it was not distressing her, it did impair her hearing. I was given drops to put in her ears daily and soon she had a recall to be proud of.

The lesson to learn from that incident was that when a problem appears and seems totally out of character with the dog, it may well have a physical cause and should be investigated by a veterinary surgeon.

When people are unwell, it is not usually very difficult to get to the root of the problem, unless they are very young; human babies, rather like dogs, are unable to answer questions about their condition. Children will feel listless and appear under the weather to a greater or lesser degree; they will lose their bounce and be less active than usual.

Similarly with dogs: a healthy dog should be eager to play and run; he should be alert and aware of what is happening around him; his eyes should be bright and his coat clean and in good condition. Most dogs, at some point in their lives, become ill and require the help of a veterinary surgeon. In any event, your dog will need to go once a year for his booster injection.

The First Visit to the Veterinary Surgeon

This is most likely to be for his first vaccination at around 8 weeks of age. You can all go along. This is part of what your children should learn about caring for a dog.

Do not take the puppy into the surgery until it is your turn; *you should not take an unvaccinated puppy into a waiting room full of other dogs which may have a variety of contagious ailments.*

It is very important that this first visit to the veterinarian is as pleasant and stress free as possible for the puppy. A disturbing experience now may make a lasting impression on him. He has no knowledge of what is in store; he does not know he is about to have an injection, so try not to have a 'pitying' attitude towards him. Just be quite matter of fact and jolly. Do not feed him before you go and take a few tasty titbits. When all is finished and he is still on the table, make a fuss of him and give him a titbit. If he is feeling timid and unsure, just be quite matter of fact and jolly.

The veterinary surgeon will examine him to make sure he is fit and healthy; he will give the puppy the necessary injection quickly and with no fuss. (See photographs 10 and 11). Most puppies do not notice a thing. If there is anything you are anxious about concerning the puppy, ask the veterinary surgeon now. Take the puppy back to the car or ask someone to hold him outside while you pay.

On completion of the vaccinations, you will be issued with a vaccination certificate; keep it somewhere safe as kennels and some dog training classes will not allow your dog entry without it. *But remember, your dog is vaccinated to keep him healthy, not so that he has a passport to kennels and classes.*

Vaccinations

Your puppy needs a programme of injections that will protect him against the five major canine diseases.

Canine Distemper
This is a very serious disease caused by a virus. It is highly infectious and often fatal, and is a major disease of the dog, endemic in the United Kingdom.

Canine Viral Hepatitis
A virus infection causes this serious condition, which mainly attacks the liver. This disease is also endemic in the United Kingdom.

Leptospirosis – Two Types
This severe and very unpleasant condition attacks the liver and kidneys and frequently ends in death. This disease can affect man (one form causes Weil's disease in humans and is very serious) so it is important, from a public health point of view to keep it under control.

Parvovirus
Parvovirus is a disease which damages the bowel lining, causing diarrhoea and vomiting. It is extremely infectious and often fatal. Puppies and adult dogs suddenly develop severe gastro-enteritis, but prompt treatment may be able to save their lives. Of all the viruses, this is the most long lived in the environment and most difficult to eradicate.

Vaccines are very effective and rarely cause any side effects. Most puppies will have received some immunization from the dam's antibodies which have transferred via the placenta and are also present in their mother's milk. Although these maternal antibodies will protect the puppy for some time, it is not clear in individuals how long a puppy is protected; it could be from 6 to 12 weeks or longer and their presence could interfere with the effectiveness of the vaccines.

Your veterinary surgeon will advise you on the timing of these vaccinations; he will know the prevalence of these diseases in your area.

Therefore, a phased programme of vaccinations is given to the puppy to ensure the vaccine produces an effective response. The first is given at around 6 to 8 weeks of age and the second at 12 weeks.

Local disease conditions vary and your veterinary surgeon will calculate the best time for vaccinating your puppy in the light of these conditions. This is particularly so for Canine Parvovirus. The maternal antibodies of this disease may remain in the puppy for longer than Distemper; therefore, the puppy may have to wait a longer time until he is ready for the vaccine.

These vaccinations do not give permanent protection and your puppy must have a 'booster' injection *once a year* to ensure that the degree of protection does not fall too low.

Kennel Cough

This is due to some very infectious agents which are not necessarily caused by dogs being in kennels. Infective particles are airborne and dogs become infected by breathing in these particles. A vaccine is available which will give some protection against some of the components of this very contagious disease. The vaccine is dripped straight into the nose and protection will last about 6 months. (See photograph 12). Some boarding kennels require dogs to be vaccinated before they will be accepted.

Sickness and Diarrhoea

In puppies, either of these can be a symptom of a number of serious diseases. They should, therefore, be investigated by your veterinary surgeon.

This can of course also be true of older dogs; a telephone call to the surgery will help you decide what to do.

Worms

These are parasites which live inside the body of the dog. Most owners are shocked to think that their puppies or dogs could have worms, but nearly all puppies have worms to a greater or lesser degree.

There are two main types, roundworms and tapeworms. The roundworm, *Toxocara canis* is one which can be transmitted to man. Effective preparations are available to treat both these conditions.

Your puppy should have been wormed by the breeder before you get him, but you must continue this worming programme as puppies need to be routinely wormed until they are 6 months old. Subsequent worming at intervals as suggested by your veterinary surgeon provides good control.

Consult your veterinary surgeon about worming your puppy or older dog. He will advise you on what to do to keep your dog free of worms.

Worms and Children

You need to be sensible about worms. Your child is much more likely to become injured on the roads than become infected by the roundworm, which is the major cause of concern. It can produce a serious condition in a child but this is fortunately very, very rare. The incidence of the disease in children is so small that official figures are not kept.

Infection is certainly preventable. Simple hygiene procedures such as making sure the children wash their hands after playing with the puppy and after playing outside in the garden or park, clearing away all dog faeces as soon as they are deposited (the eggs can live in the ground for a number of years) and regularly worming your dog, will guard against infestation. Just because you do not see worms in the faeces does not necessarily mean that he has not had worms; they may be digested within your dog and passed out – not showing in the faeces, depending upon the preparation you are using.

Feeding

Like us, dogs require a well balanced diet and although they are carnivores, they do not need an all meat diet.

The breeder will have given you a diet sheet; some of the more experienced breeders are very specific and give a detailed account of what your puppy should eat, maybe until adulthood, and even include suggestions for ways to feed him for the rest of his life. Other breeders are less detailed and it can be difficult to decide what to feed your dog on. Breeders do not need any qualifications to breed dogs and therefore the quality of nutritional information given is very variable.

A balanced diet consists of correctly proportioned amounts of protein, fat, carbohydrate, water, roughage and of course vitamins and minerals. You have a choice of two ways to feed your dog.

Homemade Diets

In the wild, carnivores will eat the whole of the animal they have caught; fur, muscle, meat and the gut, including its contents. So buying minced fillet steak for your puppy or dog and perhaps adding some biscuits will not give him all the essential nutrients he requires. It is a complicated business and difficult, particularly when feeding a puppy, to ensure he is getting all he needs. Unless you are prepared to go into thorough detail of the nutritional content of the raw material you are using and arm yourself with specific knowledge of what a dog actually requires to maintain adequate health (and growth in puppies), it is better not to embark on a feeding regime of homemade food.

Your dog will not love you more just because you have spent hours over a hot stove, lovingly preparing his food. In fact he will not notice! This time would be better spent, playing with or training him.

Commercially Prepared Foods

Proprietary foods for dogs are available everywhere; there is plenty of variety and if they are fed in accordance with the manufacturer's instructions, they are intended to provide for all the dog's nutritional needs. Many of the manufacturers have conducted a considerable amount of research, not only into dogs' nutritional requirements, but also into the foods' palatability, and provide sound feeding information.

Many dogs like variety in their food, but equally as many dogs would be happy eating the same food day after day. Their ancestors do in the wild! You decide what your dog eats, not your dog, and puppies particularly should be fed on the best you can possibly afford.

Water must always be available, regardless of what you feed to your dog.

Changing Your Dog's Diet

It is evident that some foods suit some dogs better than others. For example, dogs may have loose stools on one food and not on another; some dogs become overactive after eating a certain food. If you suspect the food may be causing problems, speak to your veterinary surgeon before you do anything about it; the symptoms may be due to other causes.

If you want to change your puppy's or dog's diet, take between 1 to 2 weeks to do this, exchanging a small portion of his original food with the new food, gradually increasing the new food. His digestive system will be upset if you change too quickly.

Quantities

How much to feed to your dog is a difficult question as it depends on how active your dog is, whether he lives inside or out and his age. Growing puppies and dogs require more food than their fully grown counterparts.

Follow the manufacturer's instructions if you are feeding a commercially prepared food and keep an eye on your dog's waistline. It is said that one third of all dogs are overweight and that means they are eating too much for their needs. It is as simple as that. They need more exercise and less food. As a rough guide, you should be able to feel your dog's ribs when you run your hand gently along his coat. If you are honest with yourself, you will know if your dog is overweight or not. A dog which is overweight is not healthy and it may shorten his life. Speak to your veterinary surgeon before putting your dog on a slimming diet; he will advise you on the best way to help your dog attain a more healthy weight.

Number of Meals

Usually a puppy of 2 to 3 months will require four meals a day; 3 to 6 months old will require three meals a day, going down to two meals at 6 months. The timing is approximate. At around 10 months to 1 year, dogs may be having one main meal and one smaller meal, usually being fed after your breakfast and after your supper at around 6 p.m.

The timing is according to your convenience, but dogs appreciate a routine and are more settled if their mealtimes are fairly regular. Many dogs are fed one meal a day from 1 year of age onwards; however many pet dogs are more content if fed two meals as described.

Fussy Eaters

Some healthy dogs are said to be finicky over their food. This problem may be caused by three reasons:

1. If the dog does not eat his 'normal' food, many owners become worried and will therefore add something to the bowl that they know he likes. This has the effect of praising the dog for not eating what you first gave him.
2. The dog has had too many treats and titbits and he is not hungry.
3. He may have had a lot of attention and concern bestowed upon him for not eating and this also provides praise for not eating.

Healthy dogs should clear the dish within a few minutes. The solution is as follows:

1. The dog's meals should be given at the same time each day.
2. Any food left after 10 minutes is to be taken away and no more food given until the next regular mealtime. No titbits either!

Feeding the Dog From Your Table

Giving him titbits while you are eating is not to be done. No pack leader dog would allow a subordinate to take bits of food while he is eating. You are, or should be, the pack leader in your dog's eyes.

If the dog is *never* given food from the table, he will not expect it. The temptation is to 'give him a bit to keep him quiet' or to 'make him go away'. Would you go away if people were giving you something nice?

And look at it from the dog's point of view; if he is waiting (or drooling) and is eventually given a tasty morsel from your plate, as far as he is concerned, that is a good reason for having waited, or barked, or nudged your elbow, or 'pawed' your leg. Never do it and the problem will never arise.

Approaching Your Dog During His Meals

The old saying that you should leave a dog alone when he is eating is simply not true. All subordinates allow their pack leaders to approach (and take away if they so wish) their food.

In the wild, if a subordinate approaches a pack leader while he is eating, he will get a growl or a snap; but if a pack leader approaches a subordinate, the subordinate will simply back off. You must be able to approach your dog while he is eating (see photograph 13); you should be able to put your hand in his bowl and take the bowl away if you want. The best way to do this is to get the puppy used to people (children and adults), stroking him while he is eating and to add a couple of titbits – different from what he has in his bowl – actually as he is eating. Like this, hands near the bowl mean something pleasant. Take the bowl away occasionally and add something, giving it back quickly. If you always take the bowl away, it may make him feel he has to defend his food.

Neutering – Castration and Spaying

Ask yourself the question, 'Do we want to breed from our dog?' In Britain there are about 1 million puppies born each year and possibly half are unplanned and unwanted. Unless you have definite plans to breed, you should consider having your dog neutered.

Castration

This is an operation which is carried out under general anaesthetic and involves the removal of the testicles. In the United Kingdom, it is usually carried out for medical and behavioural reasons.

Sexual Urges

The majority of dogs are kept as pets and companions. Dogs cannot be told off for wanting bitches in the park and as there are so many unwanted dogs, it is better to prevent further additions to the dog populations by having your dog castrated.

Benefits

Castrated dogs lose some of the pack leader behaviour, such as urinating in the house and fighting other dogs (unless he is a nervous fighter in which case castration has no effect). Castrated dogs become more inward looking because they are less inclined to roam after bitches; and this makes them easier to own and train. All male Guide Dogs are castrated at about 9 months of age.

Your dog will not know he has been castrated. Castration does not make dogs fat, although it does alter their metabolism and therefore they require less food. Castrated dogs do not become lazy. The difficulty is that the time many dogs are castrated coincides with their being more mature and they naturally become less playful. Many owners stop playing with their dogs at this time. It is this, rather than castration, which makes them less playful. Continue playing with your dog and he will remain playful until old age forces a less active life.

Age to Castrate

Most of the problems of entire (uncastrated) dogs become evident when they start to lift their leg to urinate. Discuss the best age to castrate with your veterinary surgeon.

Spaying

Most bitches come on 'heat' twice a year. During the three weeks or more of their 'season', they need to be kept apart from other dogs, bearing in mind they will have an urge to mate and may try to escape.

Spaying involves the removal of the ovaries and the womb under general anaesthetic. Although it is a major operation, recovery is usually rapid. The most important reason for spaying bitches is the prevention of unwanted puppies. However, owning a spayed bitch will be easier in that she will not have to be kept in twice a year. There are certain health advantages dependent upon the age she is spayed, such as a reduced chance of developing mammary tumours, false pregnancies and uterine problems. The emotional behaviour of the bitch usually alters during a season. They may just become more excitable or even snappy. These mood swings usually diminish after spaying.

Age to Spay

There is some controversy about the best age to spay. Some advocate the operation before the first season and some after. Your veterinary surgeon will advise you about the best age to neuter your bitch.

Spaying does not make bitches fat, although it does alter their metabolism. There are many unspayed bitches which are overweight. Bitches, like dogs, become less active as they grow into adulthood and therefore may put on weight; but less food and more play and exercise will keep her trim. Contrary to popular belief, there is no benefit to the bitch in allowing her one litter of puppies. This is an old wives' tale!

Keeping Your Dog Healthy

When your dog is taken for his annual booster injection, the veterinary surgeon will examine him; however, a year is a very long time in a dog's life.

It is essential that you examine your dog regularly (weekly with an older dog), firstly in order to make sure he is in good condition and secondly to get him used to being handled. When you are grooming him (see page 59) is a convenient time to do this. He should start getting used to this as soon as he is settled in your pack. When examining your dog you need to look at the following:

1. **Ears**: these should appear clean and odour free. Do not poke anything down – just look.

2. **Eyes**: eyes should be bright with no discharge.

3. **Mouth**: gently lift his lips to look at his teeth. They should be clean. Open his mouth by gently squeezing his lips into his gums just behind the two canine teeth (two fang teeth either side of his top jaw). Look at the inside of his teeth. There should be no tartar.

4. **Body**: go over his body to check for any abrasions. Lift his tail and feel inside his hind legs. This is the most intrusive area from the dog's point of view and he must get used to this.

5. **Paws**: pick up each paw in turn and examine to ensure they are free from cracks and grit. Look at the claws – do they need clipping?

If you get him used to being handled from an early age, he is more likely to accept a veterinary surgeon examining him and he will be more content to be handled and stroked by others.

A healthy puppy or dog should appear happy and interested in his surroundings. He should be alert and moving well without limping, he should eat well and regularly pass consistently formed motions. By observing your dog when he is healthy, and not ignoring changes, you will sense when your puppy or dog is not well and with the help of your veterinary surgeon you will learn how to deal with some of the more common, minor ailments and those that require his expert attention. If you are at all concerned about your dog's health, go to your veterinary surgeon; he should be willing to help you and learning from his expertise will ensure you are doing the best for your pet.

CHAPTER · 6

The Puppy's First Weeks with You and Your Children

WHEN Wally came to our family, he was the tiniest, most cuddly ball of fur. He had legs like other dogs but you would never have known, as he spent so much time on various laps. When Wally was allowed to use his little legs, he would go into the garden; he loved it in the garden. He would catch the raindrops if it was raining (yes, there was drinking water available all the time!); chase flying bits if it was windy; sit under the trees if it was sunny; or simply play with the children.

Wally was and still is very playful. He would run after anything they threw, but would not bring it back. I suspect he would have even chased after them, given half the chance. The children learnt that games with bouncy puppies can quickly get out of hand if allowed to. They also learnt that when it was time to come in, that had to be as much fun for Wally as staying outside; otherwise he would stay out! At first it was not easy to help the children to see that he was a dog and not a cuddly toy. Although they have lived with two dogs all their lives, for them this was their first puppy.

Wally spent a lot of time in the car. Each time I took the children to school, he came with us. He remained on his own in the car whilst I took my other dogs for their walks. Only once did he defecate in the car and I am ashamed to admit that it was my fault for leaving him too long.

I took him wherever I could carry him – to the hairdressers, post office and school playground. I wanted him to become accustomed to what was becoming his lifestyle, as soon as possible.

The Right Way From the Start

Children can learn the right way as quickly as they can learn the wrong way. They need to be shown that the right way produces good results quickly and with more fun. Children need to be constantly helped to see that what is fun in a puppy, may not be such good fun in an older, larger dog. They also need to realize that a puppy they know well, which is chasing and perhaps yapping in excitement, may not go down so well with their friends who do not know the puppy as they do.

If you approach the upbringing of your puppy in the right way from the start, the children will know no other way. The first weeks set the scene for them as well as for the puppy.

Titbits

Most pet dogs, particularly when they are young, are cuddled and stroked all day. Usually far too much. They do not have to do anything for it. They are petted lovingly, just for existing. To get them to obey you when they are having a lovely time in the garden, you need to have something extra to make them want to obey immediately. It can be toys or titbits. Usually puppies have many toys lying around and even if one is being played with for chase or tug-of-war games, it will not be special enough at the beginning. Food which is not available all the time (see page 43) can be made special. Using food as a reward is not seen as bribery to a dog. When I take my children to the supermarket and buy them crisps to keep them happy, I am bribing them. They know I am bribing them. But dogs do not have a sense of what is right or wrong. *If there is something in it for them, they will do it. If there is nothing in it for them, they will not do it.* It is as simple as that.

The rules for using titbits must be observed:

1. The reward must be given within 1 or 2 seconds of the dog having done what you have told him to do. It is no good calling him in from the garden, slamming the door and then fumbling about in the cupboard for a titbit. It is too late. As far as he is concerned, he will be getting it for hanging around in the kitchen; he will have forgotten all about coming in.
2. The titbits must never be given for nothing. He must earn every crumb he gets. The only exception to this is at the very beginning or if you are changing titbits. Give him one to show him what you have got.
3. The puppy must want the titbits. He must like what you have to offer. Try to avoid using the food he has for his meals; cheese, bits of chicken or even different dog biscuits are fine. Chocolate drops are fine, but they melt in your hand. If a titbit seems to lose its special

appeal, change to another; tuna for example – messy but dogs love it!

4. Only give tiny amounts. Quarter the size of a new 5p piece is sufficient. You do not have to give him ½ lb of stilton each time he does what you want. However, the children may require slightly bigger pieces as their little fingers are not in as much control as ours are.

5. The puppy must never jump up for titbits: bend down to him. He should only get it when *four* paws are on the ground.

6. Once your puppy is responding 100 per cent of the time, gradually and randomly cut the titbits down until he is getting one every now and then. This 'random reward' system works because reward becomes unpredictable and therefore the puppy will always try hard in the hope of getting one. He should always get praise, but sometimes he gets praise and a titbit.

Having now learnt the rules, you can use them to play the 'Recall Game' (see page 56).

Games

All puppies love to play games. So do all children. Put the two together, unsupervised, and you are likely to get problems. Puppies have four legs; they may be small, but they are speedy. Children have two legs; not nearly so speedy, but with two ankles which may be fun to chase and nip.

Puppies love to roll about on the floor. So do children. The two, playing this game together may present difficulties in teaching the puppy that he is subordinate to the children, not their equal. Many puppies love to play a game of tug-of-war, particularly the more dominant ones (see page 99) and a child can be a very willing partner. Tug-of-war cannot be played by a puppy on his own. But who usually 'wins' the article? If you are not careful, the puppy will win each time. He will then think he is the greater. Games usually start once the puppy is settled and confident in his new home. Each game teaches the puppy something different. It is important that the puppy learns the correct lessons from the games that are played with him. Otherwise, problems easily develop. Children can still play with puppies. They should play with them. It is fun and an excellent way of teaching the puppy.

Instead of negatively saying to the children 'No, do not play,' give the children something positive to do; show them how to play the right way. They will soon see it is just as much fun, if not more so, as they, the children, are in control of what is happening. Children of around 8 or 9 years of age can play these games, under supervision to start with. Younger children should always be supervised.

Chase

Chasing is great fun for many puppies and older dogs, particularly Border Collies, but far too many will chase anything that moves. No puppy should be allowed to chase children excitedly around the garden, or indoors, however much fun they all seem to be having. Similarly, under no circumstances should the children encourage the puppy to chase them inside or outside. Being chased can be as much fun for a puppy as chasing. But he will be far too quick to be caught and chasing to try and catch him in the woods, when he is allowed to go there, is not fun at all when it is time to go home. If your puppy wants to be chased, just walk away from him.

Rules

1. When the puppy is out with the children, the children must play quietly, either by themselves or with the puppy. (If they want to 'let off steam', put the puppy away from them.)

53

2. If they want to play with the puppy (one at a time), they need to play from a relatively static position.

3. They should select one toy that they know the puppy likes, shake it near the ground to encourage the puppy to want it and throw it for him to chase. Do not use the word 'Fetch' at this stage; he may associate it with running towards a toy rather than picking it up and bringing it back to you.

4. If he brings it back, praise him, wait until he drops it and throw it again.

5. If he does not bring it back, under *no* circumstances are the children to chase him. They must stay where they are and wait until he drops it. When he does, they can go and get it, return to the spot they originally threw it from, encouraging the puppy to want it and throw it again. He may keep taking it back to the same place, in which case, the children, having thrown the toy, go and wait, bending down, at that spot. If the puppy brings it to that spot, they should give him lots of praise and again wait until he drops it. Repeat No. 3.

6. Stop before the puppy becomes bored, (see page 64, Training Hints), remembering that they have a very short attention span. You want his last memory of the game to be one of excitement and pleasure, rather than boredom.

7. That is the only toy you or the children use when playing with the puppy. This toy will become special. He can have access to other toys, and although you must be able to get them off him (everything

belongs to the pack leader!), the special toy is the only one you use when playing with him. Put it away at the end of the game.

8. Chasing anything else is stopped; either use prevention or 'Aaah!'. What you are telling him is that he can chase as he seems to enjoy it so much, but only what you allow him to. Stop him chasing altogether and he may find other even less desirable outlets for his instincts – such as joggers or cars!

Channelling his instinct in this way can create a game that is enjoyable for the participants and remains under control.

Tug-of-War

Tug-of-war is a game of dominance. If you have a submissive puppy, he may not play this game at all. It is a game played to find out who is the most dominant. The dominant one always wins. Bearing in mind that the puppy thinks that all of us are animals, if he always plays this game and wins, he will feel more dominant than he should. If he likes this game, there is no need to stop him, but you must observe certain rules. It can be played with practically anything, but is usually played with a rubber ring. The rules are as follows:

1. The game should be initiated always by humans, not the puppy.
2. The puppy should not win the game. This means that he must not be the one who retains the article. You get it from him by gently, but firmly, opening his mouth and quickly saying 'leave' or 'give'. There is no need to shout. He is not deaf!
3. At the end of the game, put the toy away. It is 'your' toy to play with with him. Not his toy!
4. *There should be no growling at all.* Any growling and the game is immediately stopped, by taking the toy out of his mouth (see page 48, Keeping Your Dog Healthy) with a quiet command of 'leave' or 'give' and the toy is then put away until the next game.

In this way, the puppy will always feel that he is subordinate to humans; children and adults alike.

Rough and Tumble

This is a game that should *never* be played between humans and puppies (or dogs). Apart from the fact that the puppy has sharp teeth and can get too rough, it is a game that the puppy will always feel he has won. You lose the height advantage you have over your dog and the puppy never tires of the game. It teaches him to pit his strength against you and it is very difficult to keep under control. A playful nip now, becomes a serious bite as the puppy gets older.

Never allow the children to play rough-and-tumble games with the puppy. He will always feel as though he has won, and the game can easily get out of hand as the dog gets bigger

Recall

This is a very important game for your puppy to learn. It is usually classed as an exercise, but it should be as much fun for your puppy as a game. For the children, it can be another game for them to play with the dog. It should be played in conjunction with the recall training (see page 68).

One important element to remember: *you can never make a puppy (or a dog) that is running free come back to you. You can only make them want to come back to you* and to do that, you must have something that they want.

A child of any age can play this, but with children of under 7 or 8 years of age, an adult may stand behind the child to help him. These are the rules of the game:

1. Give each participant a few titbits and stand in a circle, or opposite each other if only two people are playing. (See photograph 15).
2. One person calls the puppy in a lovely, friendly voice, saying the puppy's name and 'Come'. If they are tall, then bending down or getting on their haunches is more welcoming for the puppy. Hold the titbits so that he can see what you have got.
3. When the puppy comes, he can immediately have the titbit.
4. The next member calls, in the same enthusiastic voice and immediately the puppy comes he gets the titbit, and so on.

Very young children might be apprehensive of giving the puppy a titbit for fear of the needle sharp teeth. Help them to hold out their hand flat, your hand underneath and keep it still as the puppy approaches. The person who calls the puppy is the only one to give the titbit. Like this, the puppy is associating his name and the word 'Come' with fun and pleasantness. Avoid boredom. Do not go on for too long. Keep fun in the game.

In addition to the puppy's life with the children, he also has a host of other new experiences to come to terms with.

Socializing

Before puppies are 16 weeks old, they need to come into contact with as many of the types of situations that will surround their lives as possible; and the experience they have in these situations *must* be associated with pleasure.

Although he cannot go where other dogs go, such as the park and training classes, before he is vaccinated, your puppy can still be exposed to many situations, as long as he is carried. Speak to your veterinary surgeon about this and the instance of disease in your area.

School

If you have children of school age, carry the puppy to school as often as you can before he gets too heavy. Allow the children to stroke him gently; no teasing or poking fingers. Get him used to the hustle and bustle of children going to and coming out of school. The children can give him a titbit.

Public Places

Although there are many places where dogs are not allowed, fortunately, there are still many places where you may take your puppy. Post

Offices and banks for example. Some hairdressers and barbers may allow them in, as may some off-licences. The adults there may be willing to give him a titbit.

Traffic
Your puppy needs to get used to heavy traffic if you live in an urban area and farm animals and tractors if you live in the country. Carry him in these areas. Use food to help him to have pleasurable associations.

At Home
All sorts of people come to your home. Your puppy needs to get used to them. Postmen, milkmen, dustmen, gas men and window cleaners. People carrying bags and wearing hats; babysitters, very important if you use them a lot; and your children's friends. Keep an eye on these friends, to make sure their behaviour towards the puppy is as you wish, gentle and not tormenting. Noises like vacuum cleaners and washing machines may not have been introduced to him by his breeder. Introduce them now; also camera flashes if you use them frequently. Think of your life; what is your puppy going to have to learn about it?

In all situations which are new to your puppy, your attitude should be matter of fact and positive. Under no circumstances should you either chastize him if he is showing fear, or comfort him. Telling him off will only make him more fearful and comforting him will seem to him as though you are praising him for being fearful.

Fearful Behaviour
If he shows apprehension in any situation, do not force him into his fear. He needs to be given confidence that the situations or people will not harm him.

Fear of People
Many puppies can be slightly fearful of certain people. This can be a bit upsetting, as we all want people to admire and stroke our dogs.

If your puppy hangs back, let him. Do not force him to make friends. Instruct the person to ignore the puppy completely; not to look at or try to stroke him. The puppy should be allowed to come forward himself, in his own time. The more ignoring the person is, the less threatened the puppy will feel. Sometimes, if the person throws a titbit to a greedy puppy and allows it to fall closer and closer to his own feet, the puppy can be encouraged to be rewarded for coming closer. The point is that the puppy is coming of his own accord.

Fear of Traffic

The same principles apply; do not force. Start off with quiet roads, gradually increasing the volume of traffic, and giving him titbits to make the association pleasant. These titbits should be given when the puppy is relaxed, not when he is tense or you will be rewarding his fear.

Collar and Lead

It is during these first few weeks that your dog needs to get used to a collar and lead. Do not waste time by waiting until his vaccinations are finished. It is also safer when carrying him out and about. Puppies are very wriggly.

Collar

Once your puppy is eating well and is settled, (this may take up to a week), you should introduce him to a collar (a buckle collar for a puppy, not a slip collar). Put the collar on him just before his favourite meal; take it off when he has finished. You should gradually increase the time it is left on, distracting him with a game to help him ignore it. He will scratch at first. Take no notice. He will get used to it.

Lead

Once he is used to the collar, apart from the odd scratch, attach a light lead just before he is fed. (See photograph 14). Again, take it off when he has finished, then gradually let him keep it on for longer periods; playing with him, letting him associate it with pleasure, but not putting any pressure on it at all. Let him drag it and discourage any chewing with 'Aaah!' Gradually pick it up and encourage him to follow you around the garden with a titbit or his favourite toy, generally helping him to associate you holding the lead with pleasure rather than control. If old enough and sensible enough, the children can help with this; *but under no account must they drag the puppy about.* Show them the right way and keep an eye on them.

Grooming

This is a very important aspect of teaching your puppy to be handled. This can be started as soon as your puppy is settled. Everyone should be able to groom the puppy, including the children. Even if your puppy is short haired (and will remain so) and even if your puppy smells delightful, he still needs to be groomed. It is the handling aspect which is important.

You need to be able to handle your dog whenever you want to. He must get used to this as a puppy so that when he is bigger (and stronger) he accepts being handled by you and veterinary surgeons. Dogs that are regularly groomed and handled from puppyhood, are far more likely to accept handling from other people whether vets or visiting friends, adults or children. Either put the puppy on a table or on the floor and hold him as shown; brush with a soft brush or cloth, especially made for this purpose. The intrusive areas from the dog's point of view are behind the ears, behind the front legs, under the tail and in between the hind legs (see page 48, Keeping Your Dog Healthy).

Grooming should be done each day. Any struggling or worse still any attempts to bite the brush or your fingers should be sharply reprimanded with 'Aaah!' Your puppy should stand there and accept it. Do not stop until he is accepting it. Again it has to be acceptance which stops the grooming, not his struggling. His acceptance should always be *rewarded* with something he likes. So either time his grooming so that it can be followed by a meal or play with him.

Feeding

(See page 46, Approaching Your Dog During His Meals.)

On His Own

Your life should not be ruled by your puppy. Dogs are social animals and prefer company, but your life cannot always include the dog, so as a puppy, he must become accustomed to being on his own, for some periods.

Follow the initial procedure as described on page 32, The First Morning. Accustom your puppy to being on his own when you are in. Occasionally, during the day, put him where he sleeps at night. If he is allowed to follow you around the house all the time, and have as much access to you as he wants he will become overdependent and may feel bereft when you are not there. Help the children to see that the puppy must learn to be on his own sometimes when they are in. Apart from the puppy's point of view, from their point of view it might mean that they can play with their toys on the floor in peace.

Almost all the activities between children and dogs require supervision initially; and younger children will always require a watchful eye kept upon them. They may be jealous of the attention given to the puppy and therefore be inclined to tease, poke or pull, resulting in a dog which becomes fearful of, or aggressive towards those he is supposed to love; and children who play 'Boo' a lot, have to learn that dogs do not like surprises.

However, children and dogs can live extremely happily together. Both have the energy and enthusiasm sometimes lacking in adults. These early weeks set the pattern. Do it correctly from the start and the puppy will grow to love and respect not only your children, but others' too; and children will enjoy playing with your puppy because they will know how to control the games they all enjoy.

CHAPTER · 7

Training Your Dog with Children Around

WHEN I obtained my first dog, I had no idea about training. As far as I was concerned, Nimrod was perfect, and he could do no wrong. The fact that he was out of control did not seem to matter. He jumped up at everyone, did not listen to what I told him to do and was generally over the top with his enthusiasm for life, virtually pulling my arm out of its socket every time there was a smell that took his fancy. He came back when he was called and was able to stay on his own when necessary, but that was it.

I was in the type of job where I could take him with me in the car, and he also spent some time in the office. He was wonderfully friendly with everyone, but not everyone shared my acceptance of his exuberant, do-as-you-please behaviour.

When Nimrod was six and a half months old (and still growing!) a colleague tentatively asked if I had ever thought of training him; he gently said that there were things called training classes to help people like me with dogs like him. Training classes?? I honestly had no idea; I just thought they would eventually learn by themselves not to pull and to sit when told. Yes, at six and a half months, Nimrod did not even know what 'Sit' was.

Well, after continued, subtle pressure I went along to training classes and that was the start of it all. I thoroughly enjoyed it and was hooked. It was hard work because of his age and the fact that I was starting from scratch, but soon Nimrod was doing what I wanted him to do. He was just as happy and my colleagues began to feel that he was actually a pleasure to have around. At that stage, I had no husband and no children. When Daisy joined our family, I had a one-and-a-half-year-old child and very soon after her arrival, another child on the way. I started her training well before she was 6 months old, but with such a young child, and myself getting larger by the minute, I often had the attitude that there was always tomorrow . . .! However, by 6 months old she was doing all I wanted her to do and having some fun as well!

Our children were older and at school when we obtained Wally, and although there was a lot of 'Mummy, can I do that with Wally', by four and a half to five months, Wally was doing everything that Nimrod and Daisy could do and a lot more besides. He did it for the children as well. He was the happiest little puppy and obedient with it. I started training him as soon as he was settled, within 1 or 2 days of him coming to us.

Training dogs can, and should be fun. What you are doing is teaching your dog to associate certain words with particular actions so that you can control him when necessary. The other purpose of training is to help your dog have a more enjoyable and fulfilled life in what is a human as opposed to canine society. A dog that is mentally as well as physically exercised is more content and will therefore be easier to manage as a pet. That does not mean that you have to take your dog to all sorts of places for him to meet many other dogs to give him exercise and variety; you can give him all he needs in his own home or on his normal off-lead runs in the park or woods. It can and should all come from you. Training can begin as early as you like, as soon as your dog is settled, usually within a week of him coming to you.

How Dogs Learn

Dogs learn by association. They learn to associate one word with a particular action. The actual word is not important, he will not understand it. You can teach him to 'Sit' to the word 'Bananas' if you want to and do it often enough, rewarding him within 1 or 2 seconds of him having done what you have told him to do. (But the word 'Sit' is easier for us to remember for this action.)

Consistency
This is vital when training your puppy. It is no good saying (to lie him down) 'Down' one day, and 'Flat' another, or 'Lie Down' another as your dog will *never* learn what the word is supposed to mean. He may learn to lie down, but only because you always point to the floor. This is the only action that is consistent in your dog's eyes.

Who Should Train the Puppy?

It is always said that one person should do the training. This is so that the puppy will not get too confused by too many different words and tones; but a dog is not trained in a family if he only responds to one person. Therefore, this should mean that one person undertakes the responsibilities for the training. Once the puppy appears to understand what a particular word or action is meaning to him, the person training the dog shows the other members of the family exactly what they are doing; they make sure that their commands and actions resemble, as near as possible, those used in training.

Children and Training

Dogs should learn to respond to children's commands, but the training itself is best left to the older children or the adults. Children vary tremendously, therefore the following ages can only be a rough guide: children around 11 to 12 years and over, can and should play a major role in the training of your dog. With help, they will usually go about this in a sensible and responsible manner. They can do as you do, but make sure you show them exactly what you are doing. Children around 8 years and over, can also help train the puppy, but the puppy should have a reasonable idea of what he is doing first, and these children will require more help to ensure consistency. Children younger than 8 years will require constant supervision and help. With many of these children the help required is as much in teaching them what not to do, such as teasing, as in teaching them what they should do. The general rule is that 'Mummy, can I have a go?' should be met with 'Yes, I will show you' rather than 'OK, you do it.'

Training Hints

The following hints should help your training sessions:

1. You will require endless patience.
2. Keep training sessions very short, 1 to 2 minutes for a puppy, gradually increasing this time as his attention span grows. Many short sessions a day are best.
3. Do not expect miracles. A gradual improvement over a period of time will give best results.
4. If you are having an 'off-day', do not train. Losing your temper will accomplish nothing and may make a lasting impression on your puppy.
5. Vary the places you train once he has learnt the basic command; just because he has learnt to sit for his food in the kitchen, it does not mean he will automatically sit anywhere else. He has to be taught that 'Sit' means 'Sit', anywhere you choose.
6. Do not shout at your dog. He is not deaf. A command spoken in a quiet, firm voice will make your dog listen more than if you are always shouting.

7. Praise and reward must come within 1 or 2 seconds of your puppy having done what you have told him to do. In exercises such as the 'Sit', 'Down' 'Stand' and 'Stay', praise and reward must come while he is still in the position.
8. Follow the rules for titbits on page 51 and hold titbits firmly so that he does not get them at the wrong time.
9. Your dog needs to know when the exercise is over. Release him by using a word such as 'OK' or 'Alright'. Be consistent.
10. Make training fun for your dog, he will enjoy it more and learn better. Always end on a positive note and start and end each session with a little game.

Left or Right Side?

Traditionally, dogs are trained to walk on your left side; this is so that your right hand, if you are right handed, is free to use as required. Should you decide to walk your dog on the right, that is OK, but you should decide – not your dog. However, in training classes and competitions, dogs are worked on the left, except Agility when it is beneficial to work the dog on the left and right. For simplicity's sake, the exercises are given for dogs positioned on the left-hand side. All the following exercises can be started as soon as your puppy is settled, but can also be done with older dogs. They can be done on or off the lead; however, a bouncy puppy is easier to control when on the lead.

Your puppy has been called 'Fido' in this book.

Training Exercises

Sit

This is usually the first exercise that is generally thought of when training a dog.

1. With the puppy by your leg, kneel down, hold a titbit slightly above, but very close to his nose.
2. Gently push his bottom to the ground saying 'Fido, sit' at the same time. When he sits, immediately give him the titbit and praise, before he gets up.
3. Release him with your chosen word.
4. Repeat twice.

Children Around 7 to 8 Years
The puppy should be responding quite well to you first.

1. Position child in front of you. He holds the titbit as you did.

2. Place his hand on Fido's bottom, and place your hand on top of his hand. Gently push Fido's bottom to the ground as the child says 'Fido, sit' and the child gives titbit and praise immediately.
3. Release and repeat twice.
4. Help the child to do it on his own. Repeat twice.
5. During subsequent sessions, you could do it once and the child on his own twice. Use your judgement to ensure success.

Children Around 11 Years and over
They can do as you do. Supervise as necessary.

Helping a young child
to teach the puppy to sit

Down

The word you use is important. If you use the word 'Down' to stop him from jumping up (see page 105), then you cannot use the word 'Down' for lie down. You will have to use different words for these commands. Remember that 'Get down' – stop jumping up – is usually said quite spontaneously. Telling a dog to lie down is more thought out and therefore it is easier to use a different word. Decide amongst yourselves which word you are going to use and stick to it. 'Lay' is too like 'Stay', but 'Flat' is a good word.

Down is the most submissive position; with an older dog that is perhaps dominant, you will need to reduce his dominance first, (see page 97, Who is the Boss?).

1. Put the puppy in the 'Sit' position.
2. With your puppy on your left side, kneel and place your left hand on his shoulder blades, titbit in your right hand nearly touching his nose. If necessary, put gentle pressure downwards with your left hand and *at the same time* move the titbit from his nose, straight down to the floor, sweeping it in an 'L' shape; but not too far along the floor, otherwise he will have to get up to get it. Command 'Fido, flat' as he goes down.
3. Give him praise and titbit immediately, while he is still down.
4. Release him with 'OK' (or whatever word you have chosen).
5. Repeat twice.

Children Around 7 to 8 Years

The puppy should be responding quite well to you first.
1. From the sit position, both of you at Fido's side, child's hand on Fido's shoulder blades, your hand directly on his. The child holds the titbit as you did. You may need to hold his 'titbit hand' as well, the first few times.
2. You push gently with your left hand, and at the same time, help the child to move the titbit from Fido's nose to the floor in an 'L' shape. Command 'Fido, flat' as he goes down.
3. Release and repeat again.

Helping a young child to teach the down

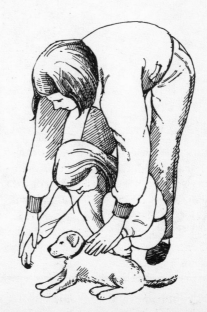

4. Help the child do it on his own twice. During further sessions, you and your child could do it once and then your child on his own, twice. Use your judgement to ensure success.

Children Around 11 years and over
They may need some help as for 7 to 8 year olds.

Recall (Come to Me Now) – at Home

The recall game (see page 56) needs to be reinforced; because in addition to the game, you need to call your dog from time to time in the house, in the garden and ultimately in the park.

1. Start by calling him, using his name and the word 'Come', when you know he will come anyway. Run backwards, away from him as he approaches you to encourage him to come quickly. Always give him praise and a titbit. Ensure success every time to get him into good habits.

2. When he is coming well, gradually start calling him when he is doing other things, such as generally sniffing around and playing, but not when playing too excitedly at first. Build it up gradually. Ensure success at each stage.

3. If he does not come (and he should only refuse once), go up to him and put the titbit right under his nose. Enticing him with the titbit,

run backwards, encouraging him to come with you to where you originally called him, giving him the titbit as you both arrive at the spot. For persistent ignoring, try changing to a much more exciting titbit, before a meal when he should be hungry or use a squeaky toy kept especially for this exercise. If he still ignores you, put on his lead and use this to encourage him to come to you, in conjunction with all the above.

4. Gradually increase the distractions.
5. To him, his name should always be associated with pleasure from you. *Never* call him to you for a telling off; he will only be reluctant to come next time. Also never make a grab for him; this will teach him to get out of the way more quickly.
6. He should allow you to get hold of his collar, however; that is what you will need to do in the park and it must be associated with pleasure. As he reaches you, gently stroke him round the collar region and equally gently get hold of his collar. Reward him immediately with praise and a titbit and freedom again.
7. Ensure that his name remains meaningful to him. If you all use his name endlessly, not expecting any response from him, he will learn that it is just part of the background burble coming from your mouths that he ignores anyway. Children can be particularly prone to overusing his name.
8. Although he cannot go to the park until his inoculations are complete, this teaching must start now. *If he will not come to all of you willingly and immediately in this familiar environment, he is unlikely to come to you when running free in the park.*

Stand

This is generally used when grooming and to enable vets to examine your dog with greater ease. This exercise is easier to do with the dog on the lead:

1. With your dog in the 'Sit' position, hold titbit in right hand in front of his nose.
2. With the left hand, palm facing downward, placed just behind his ribs under his stomach, gently lift his back end up. Command 'Stand' as you raise him. Keeping your left hand in position, praise him and give him the titbit whilst he is still standing.
3. Place left hand gently on his bottom – 'Sit' and praise him.
4. Repeat twice.

Teaching the puppy to stand

Walking to heel

Children
Young children may find this difficult, but 11 year olds and older can be shown how to do this.

Walking to Heel
'Heel' means walking on a slack lead with his shoulders roughly parallel to your leg. It is most important that your dog never gets used to pulling on the lead. He is never to get anywhere by pulling. Do not wait to start this exercise until he is allowed to walk on the street. You can start in the garden and house. Your puppy must be used to a collar and lead first. There are two basic methods of teaching a dog to walk to heel. One involves giving reward, the other involves correction and reward. You can use either, or both with a puppy.

Reward
This method of teaching a dog to walk to heel is as follows:

1. Hold the lead in the right hand and titbit in the left hand, quite low down for the puppy. Keep the titbit near your leg.
2. Walk, keeping the lead loose saying 'Fido, heel' as you set off.
3. Because of the titbit, the puppy should still be with you after a couple of paces. Reward him with praise and a titbit and continue.
4. Do not go on too long. Stop while the going is good.
5. Practise frequently for very short periods.
6. If you find that your puppy gets overexcited and tries to jump up for the titbit, first of all hold it tightly so that he cannot get it, secondly just stop. Wait patiently until he is calm and start again. When he is calm and you can take even one step, give him a titbit to reward that behaviour immediately.

Correction and Reward
This is the method usually used in the street. Using titbits to train the dog when you may have a pushchair as well, is difficult. It can be also used in the house or garden however.

1. Hold the handle of the lead in the right hand; your left hand is used for correcting. The lead must be slack but not too long.
2. Start to walk as you say 'Fido, heel', and the second the puppy pulls, put your left hand on the lead, and change direction away from his pull. Do this gently and use an encouraging tone of voice.
3. When the puppy is with you, *immediately* take your left hand off the lead so that it goes slack again and praise.
4. In the first session, practise until you can go a very short way on a slack lead.

5. This exercise requires practice like any other. The distractions may be greater however, because the puppy is always reaching new places and smells.

Children

The co-ordination and timing required to teach this to the dog is too great for younger children. For older children, help the puppy to respond reasonably to you before you teach them, attaching a second lead for you to hold, if done on the street.

Stay

'Stay' to the dog will mean stay in one position, on one spot until you go back to him. So if you are going to leave him in places such as the car, or in the house, do not say 'Stay'; in those situations it does not matter if he stands on his head during your absence – he does not have to stay in one position on one spot. *Your puppy must never get up when he wants to, only when you release him.* He must be praised before you release him, while he is still in position. If he gets more praise once he has got up, he will feel getting up is better.

1. Have several titbits in your right hand, lead held in left hand. Place dog in 'Sit' at your side.
2. Hold titbit in front of him. Command 'Stay' and you stand up straight, remaining at his side.
3. Repeat 'Stay', praise him and give him a titbit.
4. Count to two, repeat 'Stay' and give him another titbit.
5. Praise him again, and release him by getting him off the spot. *No more praise once he is released.*
6. Repeat twice.
7. When he is doing that well, and sitting for 5 to 10 seconds, do as above, but you should swivel in front of him, instead of remaining at his side, gradually increasing the time and your distance.
8. Should he jump up for the titbit at any time, you must place him back into the sit position. *He is not to get a titbit unless he is actually doing what you want.*
9. Once he is beginning to understand 'Stay', in the 'Sit' position teach him the 'Down Stay'. The method is exactly the same.

Children

Younger children should be discouraged from using 'Stay' indiscriminately. It is very easy for them to say 'Stay' to the puppy when what they may mean is 'stop jumping up' for example. Children of eleven years old and over can do as you do, but will require help and supervision to start with.

Teaching the puppy to stay

Children Around 7 to 8 Years
The puppy should be responding quite well to you first, then do the 'Stay' exercise with the child, positioning the child in front of you and making sure the child's hand with titbit is kept *still*.

Games

Hide and Seek
This can be classed as a game, but it teaches the puppy to find someone when he cannot see them. He needs to be reasonably good at coming when called first. Start inside.

1. One person holds the puppy (the holder) in a room while the other (the caller) leaves, showing the food reward to the puppy and goes just out of sight, round a corner.
2. When he is in position, he immediately calls the puppy and the holder commands 'Seek' and lets the puppy go. He should not push the puppy.
3. When the puppy has found the caller, he is immediately given much praise and a titbit by the caller.

73

4. If the puppy has any difficulty, he should be helped to find the caller.
5. Repeat twice in the same place.
6. Gradually make it more difficult for the puppy, playing inside and out, varying the places. However, he should always be rewarded by finding the person, so do not proceed too fast. This is fun for children.

Hunting

In the wild, our dogs' ancestors had to hunt for their food; although our dogs retain some of these hunting characteristics, we do the hunting for them each time we shop for their food. Dogs love to hunt. Their sense of smell is infinitely greater than ours and it is satisfying for them to be able to use it.

1. Start in a room where there is a fair amount of furniture, tables and chairs and so on.
2. Someone should hold the puppy, whilst someone else places a titbit just behind a chair leg perhaps. Let the puppy watch.
3. The puppy is told 'Find' and allowed to go and find the titbit. He will probably go straight there, having used his eyes rather than his nose at first, but that is OK. Praise him when he gets it and help him if required.

4. Repeat 2 to 3 times, putting the titbit in different places and he will get the idea very quickly.
5. Gradually make the 'Find' more difficult by initially letting him see where you are putting it but turning him around before sending him.
6. Sometimes pretend to put the titbit down, but then place it elsewhere.
7. You will soon reach the stage where you can put the titbit down without him seeing where and he will then find it.
8. This can also be played outside, hiding the titbit in long grass or behind a tree. Make sure the titbit is crunchy so that you know when he has found it. Otherwise he may quickly swallow it and go on sniffing. Praise and repeat.
9. He must be rewarded with a find each time. Even quite young children can be involved in this as they can be the ones to hide the titbit.

The day will eventually arrive when he is allowed to go where other dogs go. This is usually much looked forward to.

Collars and Leads

By this time your puppy should be well used to a collar and lead, but many people feel that just because he is now allowed out, he has to have something different. Although there are many different collars and leads available, there is no need to change unless you feel his collar, for instance, is not really strong enough.

Check chains are most commonly thought of, particularly with larger breeds, but they are not obligatory *and should never be used on a puppy*. Half checks (see illustration on the next page) can provide more control than ordinary collars. Head collars give excellent control with some dogs, particularly those of large or heavier breeds that owners have found difficult to train to walk to heel.

Your dog's ordinary collar should be fitted so that you can get two fingers inside quite easily and he cannot slip out of it. With some breeds it may need to be tighter to ensure he cannot slip out of it; English Bull Terriers, for example, have wide necks and relatively narrow heads. Half checks may be a good compromise for these dogs. The lead should be long enough for you to hold comfortably. A chain lead is not necessary; not only does it hurt your hands, it can also knock his face as he is walking. Chewing of the lead can be very quickly discouraged with an appropriate taste deterrent applied to the lead. The more expensive the lead, the more firm you will be in stopping this bossy behaviour!

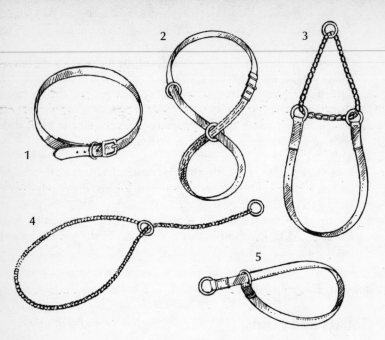

1 Buckle collar 2 Figure-of-eight head collar 3 Half-check 4 Check chain 5 Nylon slip collar

The First Outings

The First Walk

Do as you did in the garden, using the correction and reward method, remembering that he will be very distracted on the first occasion. However, discourage him from pulling and deciding which side he walks on, darting from one side to the other at will. Keep the lead fairly short, but loose.

If your puppy seems generally timid and appears so on his first walk, do not force him. Carry him out of the gate and a little way up the road and then let him walk back. Encourage him to come to you with a titbit. Do not go back and cuddle him, this will praise his fear and do not drag him either. *Your dog should never be off the lead on the street, however well trained he becomes.* Dogs are animals and can forget their training and be across the road in seconds.

The First Visit to the Park

This is always eagerly looked forward to, but many owners are anxious

Never drag the puppy on the lead

Bend down and encourage him to come to you with a titbit

about letting their puppy off the lead for the first time. Will he come back? *If he is not coming back to you in the house and garden, he will not come back to you in the park* where there are even more distractions. Review the 'Recall' training.

During the first couple of visits to the park, keep him on the lead, just watching his reactions; and keep an eye open for the kind of dogs that go there. Are there many strays? Or do most of the dogs have owners around? However, you have to realize that most dogs are friendly and have no intention of savaging your puppy, in the same way that most drivers do not knock into you when you are driving. But you need to be aware of other dogs as it is important that the encounters he has with them are friendly. A nasty meeting when he is young may make him nervous of dogs for the rest of his life. When he is to be let off the lead, take his favourite titbits with you and make sure he is a bit hungry. In any case, you should always take him out before, rather than after, his meal. Let him see what you have, give him a bit and let him off. He will probably not go very far away the first time, being perhaps a little unsure. If he does have a run and sniff around, do not call him all the time. This only makes him ignore the sound of your voice. Make your 'calls' meaningful and only call him once, when you want him to come.

Call him from time to time, when you know he is going to come; bend down, give him lavish praise, stroking around his collar, give him a titbit and let him go straight off again. Allow him to enjoy himself and encourage him to follow you by walking purposefully in different directions and calling at the same time. Most puppies do not want to be left!

Do not always put the lead on in the same place. When calling him back for the last time, put the lead on casually, giving him another titbit once the lead is attached and walk away from the gate at first so that he does not think he is going home the minute the lead is on.

Remember that you can only make a dog *want* to come back to you; if the only play your dog gets is from other dogs, you are going to become second best. He must get fun and play with you mostly. Coming back to you should be fun. Sometimes, take his 'special' toy with you. Have a little game in the woods, but stop while he is still excited and continue your walk. Occasionally, hold him and throw or place a titbit in long grass, then send him to find it (see page 74, Hunting). *If you give him fun, he will want to stay with you.*

Settling Him Down

Around the time when he is allowed out, many puppies become active and demanding, just when you want to relax. When you are busy, he knows that it is no good pestering as he never gets played with; but in the evening he knows equally well that if he pesters persistently enough, someone will oblige. This soon loses its entertainment value and becomes a tiring nuisance. The children are in bed and you do not want to have to play with this animal. He must be played with, that is one of the major ways you build a relationship with him, but it must be when you want. Make time available for it.

There are two solutions:

1. Ignore him completely. Any demand is met with nothing from you. No words to 'Go away' and no push to physically help him on his

way. Nothing! *Remember, if there is nothing in it for him, he will stop the behaviour.*

2. Put him on the lead and put your foot on it, ignoring him at the same time. He will eventually settle down.

Most restless puppies benefit from an enforced period of settling down, half an hour – three times a week, or every day for a puppy which is constantly rushing around. For some puppies, the more you command them to lie down, and try to make them obey, the more active they become. This is because he is getting a lot of attention in the process. It may be negative attention to you, but to him it may be better than nothing. That is why ignoring works so well. Remember, if there is nothing in it for him, he will stop doing it. Therefore put him on a lead and place your foot on it; do not keep talking to him or petting him and keep the lead short enough so that it is more comfortable for him to lie down – but do not squash him into the floor. Then you do nothing else but read this book in peace.

After a few protesting struggles, he will settle down and may even go to sleep. The important point is that he should not be allowed to get up until you decide and that is only when he is settled, otherwise he will think that the more he struggles, the quicker he can get up.

Training Classes

If you want to join classes, there is no need to wait until the dog is 6 months old. Many places now, quite rightly, take puppies as soon as their inoculations are complete. Joining a good class can be a rewarding experience for you and your dog. Unfortunately, some classes leave a lot to be desired. Before joining a class you should consider the following:

1. Visit as many classes as you can before you enrol. Go without your dog and watch.
2. Do the people and dogs appear relaxed, or is there a lot of noise, dogs barking, people shouting and general over excitement? Is the atmosphere friendly? Someone should greet you as you come in, for example, and no one should be made to feel embarrassed over the behaviour of their dog.
3. Do the instructors appear to know what they are talking about? Can they enable the handlers to pass this on to their dogs? Just because they have superbly trained dogs of their own, it does not mean they can teach other people. The skills required are different. People need to be shown what to do, preferably with their own dog or one of similar size and/or temperament. Just telling them is not good enough.
4. How large are the classes? In the beginner classes of more than around 8 to 10 handlers and dogs, it is simply not possible for one person to give the individual attention that some people may require. All dogs are different and while most of what is taught will suit most dogs and handlers, inevitably some will require a different approach. In larger classes, there should be an assistant to the instructor; and that person must have the same approach to training so as not to confuse the handlers (and dogs). Each person should go away from the class knowing exactly what they have to do with their own dog. If they do not get it right in class, they will not get it right at home.
5. There are different methods of training dogs, some are kinder than others. Would you be happy to do with your dog what the class members are being told to do with theirs?
6. Do they allow children (11 year olds and older) to train in class? Many children enjoy going to training class (as long as the dog is not too large for them to manage) and it can become an absorbing hobby. Some children will require extra help and patience; this needs to be available in class. (See photographs 16 and 17).

The most important aspect of training a dog is that it should be fun for dog and handler alike. In our society, a dog which is not well trained, is a misery to himself and those around him.

Training need not be very time consuming and for a relatively little input of time and effort, you will be rewarded with a wonderful companion, who is eager to please, content with his life and a joy to own.

CHAPTER · 8

Introducing Children and Dogs to One Another

WHEN I had our second child, I already had two dogs and having successfully introduced one dog to a new baby, I never gave a moment's thought to repeating the process.

Although the dogs slept downstairs, they were allowed all over the house and that was not to change when the baby arrived. There was, however, one major situation I had overlooked: nappy changing. With our first child, we were in a different house and the arrangements for this frequent activity were more suitable with dogs around in that there was a convenient surface upon which to put the baby while I changed his nappy. In the subsequent house, there was no such place and I had planned to use a mat laid on the floor of our new son's bedroom. Simple. But what I had not bargained for was the fact that first of all Daisy, the Springer Spaniel, tended to follow me all over the house and secondly that she might feel upset in any way by the arrival of another child. Nimrod was not at all bothered. I could have brought a pig into the house and he would have accepted it; but Daisy was altogether a different dog and was rather more unsettled about the whole business, becoming clingy and insecure.

The first time I changed our son's nappy, on the floor, there she was, long ears brushing over his face as she tried to get close to me and lie down. She has a fairly abundant, silky coat and although I am sensible and do not panic overmuch about hygiene, I felt that was going too far. I had two choices. I could either shut her out, or hastily make other arrangements for performing this necessary task which is a major activity with babies. I chose to make other arrangements, however inconvenient in that particular room. If I had shut her out, she would have become even more unsettled as her normal, everyday life would have changed. As it was, she just lay at my feet, and apart from being rather overattached to me during those first few weeks, she very quickly accepted the fact that there was another member to our pack and settled back into her normal life.

Dogs prefer routine. Even a chaotic family has a routine. Doors are either left open or closed. Meals are roughly at the same time each day, even if one family might produce more noise and mess, with more running around, to get the meal on the table. Change is not acceptable to most dogs. They need time to adjust to new situations, and that includes children.

Socializing Dogs – If You Do Not Have Children

The introduction of dogs to children is crucial to all who own dogs, whether they have children or not. Children walk in parks and woods where dogs are also walked; they play on beaches and walk on the streets. Other children deliver newspapers, help collect jumble for school fêtes and generally go about their daily lives. So all dogs should be correctly socialized with children from as early an age as possible.

If you do not have children, but are planning to have a baby, or there are children in your extended family, you need to make a concerted effort to introduce your dog, whilst it is still a puppy, to other people's children. But you have more of a reason to make this effort; those who have no children around, now or in the foreseeable future, also need to make an effort because children are part of our society and dogs cannot avoid coming into contact with them at some point.

Children are not mini adults. Their whole behaviour is more unpredictable and boisterous. Their voices are louder and more shrill. Their movements are more jerky and excitable. With an extended family who have young children, socializing your puppy may not present too much of a problem, in that the practicalities of finding children to introduce will be considerably easier.

Homes

The temptation is to leave the puppy at home when you visit so that you can have a nice quiet afternoon; but if all are agreed, take him with you. You have to watch the children to make sure their behaviour towards your puppy is as you would wish. That is:

1. No teasing or tormenting.
2. No screaming or excitable behaviour.

Alternatively, invite the children to your home. The rules are as above and if your puppy becomes overexcited in either situation, put him on the lead. Games as described in Chapters 6 and 7 can be played. When the puppy is allowed where other dogs go, take the children with you occasionally, when you take him for the walk. Watch for early signs of chasing by the puppy or children. Both should be stopped.

If there are no children in your extended family, there are still a number of ways you can socialize your puppy with children.

School Entrances

These are good places when children are arriving at or leaving school. Tell the teacher or person in charge first, or introduce yourself to some of the parents and explain why you are there. Mostly they will be captivated by the puppy and pleased to help. Stand the other side of the road if the puppy is a little bemused, remember that children are not what he is used to. Gradually get closer as his confidence increases (see page 58, Fearful Behaviour). When you get close you will find that while some children may be fearful of a bouncy puppy, many children will want to stroke him; make sure that not too many crowd round all at once and teach them how to approach a puppy, quietly and bending down if he has finished his inoculations and is allowed on the ground. Similarly, quiet strokes if the puppy is in your arms. Standing near a lollipop lady is a good place, introducing your dog to traffic and children at the same time.

Playgrounds

Not all playgrounds allow dogs entry but some are attached to parks. As playgrounds are often in areas frequented by many other dogs, you should wait until your puppy's vaccinations are complete. This is another area where children gather. Not so much in winter, although on a pleasant day there will always be one family around. During the week days, there are usually quite a number of pre-school age children enjoying themselves; running about, jumping, playing and generally making a noise. Either walk through the park or sit on a bench and relax. Your puppy will accustom himself to all these sights and sounds, familiar to you but not to him – keep him on the lead to prevent him running and chasing.

Some dogs take the hurly-burly world of children in their stride. Others need careful introduction to children from an early age, to ensure that they are accepted by the dog as part of everyday life. The association must be pleasant. This is vital.

Children's Behaviour Towards Strange Dogs

It is an unfortunate fact of life that even children who are quite used to dogs are often never taught how to behave towards the strange dogs which surround their daily lives. If there are dogs in the family, it is easy to assume that the children, having grown up with dogs, will not provoke an attack by a seemingly inoffensive dog. However much children may like dogs, not all dogs are like their own pet.

It is wise not to assume anything; teach children what they can and cannot do and explain why. Do not make them fearful, just give them reasons and they will have a better understanding. They need to understand that not all dogs bite but it is best not to take the risk. Children and unfamiliar dogs can live happily and safely together if some simple rules are observed.

Dogs on the Lead

Dogs Tied Up Outside A Shop
Children (and adults!) should never approach a dog which is tied up outside a shop, even if it is the next door neighbour's dog which they know. Dogs that are tied up often feel they are guarding the small area that surrounds them and this may include their lead, and they could therefore, become aggressive. In any case, nothing is known of the temperament of these dogs.

Dogs With Their Owners
The child must always ask for permission to stroke a dog; even when the dog is on the lead with his owner. Not all dogs are friendly or used to children, however adorable they may appear. Some dogs may also feel protective of their owners.

With permission given, some dogs may want a sniff first and then a stroke; some dogs are happier with a stroke under the chin rather than on top of the head.

Children should never force themselves upon a dog that backs off when on a lead or off the lead. (See photograph 19). This is one of the quickest ways of helping dogs acquire a fearful response towards children. If the dog does back off, any attentive advances should be stopped *immediately* and the child should stand still, not looking at or touching the dog, allowing the dog to approach the child if he (the dog) is confident enough. (See photograph 20). Otherwise the dog should be left alone. He requires a more gradual introduction to children.

Dogs off the Lead

Dogs in these situations may also appear safe to some children, but there are potential dangers with them too.

85

Dogs in Cars

When dogs are left in cars, the window is (or should be) a little open. It can be very tempting for children to put their hands in and stroke what to them may seem a lonely, forlorn dog. This should never be done, however sensitive the child is. As with dogs tied up outside shops, many feel they are guarding the car and will regard a little hand, albeit friendly, as intrusive. Also, he may not be friendly towards children.

Dogs Behind Gates

When children are perhaps riding their bicycles on the pavement, and see a dog sitting behind a gate, another tempting situation is presented to them. (See photograph 18). These dogs may also feel they are guarding or have unsound temperaments and should never be approached.

Stray Dogs

No stray dog should ever be approached by children. If they meet a stray dog (or stray dogs) the child should be helped to see that if he runs away and screams, this may excite the dogs and frighten them into chasing.

If the dog is just walking along, concentrating on his own business, that is what the children should do, concentrate on their own business and walk on, *they should not stare at the dog.* If approached by a dog, the child or children should stand still, hands by the sides and not stare at him. The dog will find this boring and should eventually go away.

Children Taking Dogs for Walks

Children should never take friends' dogs, or their own, for a walk on their own, unless they are very sensible, around 14 years of age, and the dog is well behaved and not too large to be managed. Dogs are animals and can behave unpredictably. The child needs to be strong enough to prevent being pulled across a road by the dog which wants to say hello! to a cat; and sensible enough to know what to do if a local stray makes amorous advances to the beautiful dog on the end of the lead.

Children Who are Afraid of Dogs

Unfortunately, there are an increasing number of children who are afraid of dogs. If they have been bitten, their fear is easy to understand; however, some have never been bitten.

Dogs are very much part of our society and most children will come into some sort of contact with dogs during their everyday lives. For some children who are really afraid of them, their lives can become

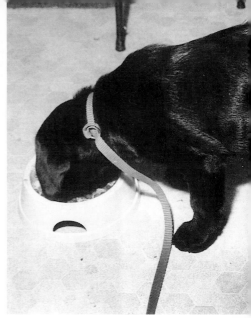

13. Dogs should allow adults and children near them when they are eating. This dog has been quite happy to eat her meal with the young boy stroking her

14. It is quite possible for a puppy to ignore the collar and lead if he is engrossed in something else and he will associate it with pleasure

15. Through the recall game, this 13-week-old puppy is learning that if she goes to the person who is calling her she will get something nice, be it a favourite toy or food

16. These dogs have been taught a variety of 'stays' at a dog training club

17. The exercise can be made fun for children to continue the training at home

18. This dog seems friendly enough but it is best not to approach unless his owner is there and has given permission

19. Having been given permission to stroke this young dog, the child approached in a typical way and the dog backed off, rather unsure

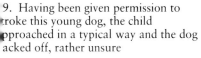

21. This is not a welcome anyone wants, however friendly it seems!

20. The young boy was given a titbit and told to step back and stand still, holding the titbit close to his body; the dog felt confident enough to approach and was rewarded for doing so

22. Putting a bouncy dog on the lead and putting your foot on it gives more control to the situation

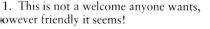

23. Let the dog investigate the new member of the pack

24. There are no young children in the families of any of these dogs, but early socialization has helped them accept being surrounded by these children who have jus come out of school

rather inhibited as they look for dogs around every corner. Forcing these children to confront their fear will not make them view dogs favourably. If I had been forced to confront Elsa (Joy Adams's lioness) all I would have wanted was for the experience to end and never to be repeated, however often I had been told that she was friendly and didn't bite! She looked lovely, but I'm sure I would have been terrified!

These children need slow, careful introductions to *very* calm dogs which do not jump up. For some, going regularly for a walk with the owner and dog (on a lead) helps to accustom them to the fact that many dogs are not really interested in them and will ignore them. Sitting in a room (as far from the dog as possible), with the dog on a lead, lying at the owner's feet may be the next step. The important factor is that the child should be quite happy at each stage before going on to the next.

Introducing an Established Dog to a New Baby

Dogs are creatures of habit and routine. They quickly get used to a certain way of life and change of any sort may upset a dog, particularly one that is sensitive.

Preparations
The time to start preparing the dog for the arrival of a baby is as soon as the pregnancy is confirmed. You should have about 7 months to bring the dog's lifestyle close to what it will be like when a baby comes home. Your dog cannot understand the fact that because you will have relatively little time for him in the future, you are going to give him extra love and affection now to make up for it. By necessity, this will suddenly diminish abruptly when the baby arrives and his behaviour will deteriorate as a result.

Time
This disappears at an alarming rate with a baby around. Your dog may have had your undivided attention. He will have been played with, taken for walks, chattered to and perhaps treated like a baby himself. Be honest with yourself. When the baby comes along, all your loving attention will be lavished upon another living being. Your dog will feel he is not getting what he has previously felt was part of his life and therefore he may become more demanding and pushy. It is surprising how many dogs become 'the dog' once the baby has arrived, as opposed to 'our Fido' as he was before.

If the dog has had your attention as and when he wanted it, start now to make time to play with him when *you* want. *You* decide when to start the games and you finish the games. Get them under your control and he will be just as happy as he is being played with, but will be less demanding as his demands are met with nothing from you. He will still need to be walked when the baby arrives, so that aspect of his life will remain unchanged. However, if someone else's help is to be enlisted for this in the early days of the baby's arrival, have him (or her) accompany you on walks to start with, gradually letting the dog be taken for walks by the new person alone, before the baby arrives.

Rooms

If your dog is allowed all over the house, whenever he wants, will you want this when the baby comes home? Will you want this when the baby is crawling on what was previously the dog's domain – the floor – with the dog slobbering over his toys? Do you want the dog in the room when you change the baby's nappy? All these questions are personal. Answer them honestly and make the required changes now.

Your dog may have to get used to being the other side of the door from where you are. Start gradually by shutting the door on him for very short periods. If you think you might sometimes keep him in the kitchen when the baby is crawling around (it may seem a long time away, but it comes all too soon) or perhaps when you are feeding your child, start now either by using a baby gate (you will need one anyway!) or closing the door. This arrangement will also give the dog a break from an overattentive child.

Sleeping Arrangements

If he is at present sleeping with you, you may want him downstairs; this must be changed as soon as possible. It will be a big adjustment for him although better for him in the long run. Dogs should not sleep in your bedroom! If he is sleeping on your bed, get him off each time he gets on. Put newspapers on the bed if you sleep deeply; the noise will awaken you (you will have a few unsettled nights) and accustom him to sleeping in a basket beside your bed. Progressively move the basket nearer to the door. When he has accepted this, put the basket outside the door and close it.

All this may take a couple of weeks or more. Then move the basket to the bottom of the stairs using the baby gate to prevent him from getting upstairs. Either leave him there or move him elsewhere downstairs. The choice is yours.

Toys

Think ahead. If your dog is used to picking up anything on the floor, because all his toys are all over the place anyway, this will not bode well when the baby's toys are scattered about. To him, they will appear to be his. His squeaky 'Prime Minister' will be the same as your baby's squeaky 'Snoopy'!

1. Pick up all his toys and put them in a cupboard. It will then become possible for you to play with him when *you* want, not when he demands.

2. Picking up anything else is to be stopped by the use of a very loud noise. Clap a couple of pan lids together making the noise loud enough to make him jump, just as he is about to put his mouth to the object. Look at it from your point of view. If each time you were about to pick up an object, you received a loud enough and sudden enough noise to make you jump, you would not do it very often. Dogs are no different in this respect.

    Some of these changes may be major ones for your dog. Proceed very gradually, allowing him to adjust to one change before embarking on the next.

Babies Crying

Apart from socializing your dog (see page 83), make a special effort to stand around outside a mother and baby clinic. These are very good places to find crying babies! You need do nothing except sit on the wall – if there is one – and your dog will become accustomed to the noise. You may like to give him a titbit as a baby cries to make the association pleasant, but be careful not to reward him if he is alarmed. It will not be the same as a baby crying in the house, but the noise will no longer be strange to the dog. You could also make a tape recording of a baby crying and play this in the house to accustom the dog to the sound.

Introductions

Your dog's life should by now have become adjusted to a style which can accommodate a new, time consuming living being. However, the first meeting is all important, as it tends to set the scene for the future.

1. Ask someone to take the dog for a good period of exercise just before the baby is brought home. He should then be tired and less excitable.

2. Remember, one member of his pack will have been away, so she will get an exciting welcome back. Have someone else hold the baby while the dog is greeted.

3. Once all this is done, and the dog has calmed down a little, he will want to sniff the new 'bundle'. Let him. Sit down with the baby (if

the dog is over exuberant then put him on his lead) and let him investigate. (See photograph 23). Draw the line at a cold nose examining the newborn baby's face, but otherwise, bottom, legs, feet, arms and back may all be examined. Just remember, we examine with our eyes, dogs examine with their noses.

4. Your dog will not go on sniffing the baby forever! He will eventually become bored. Feed him and give him a bone or other item to chew on to keep him occupied and you can then carry on with whatever you need to do.

5. You should never force your dog to 'make friends' with the baby. If he is a little wary, let him approach in his own time. A greedy dog could be given a titbit as he approaches to help him realize the baby can bring him pleasure.

6. *Never* leave your dog and baby alone without supervision, however well things seem to have gone.

Your dog regards children as other animals (he might be right!). He must be subordinate to them but he must also associate them with pleasure. Many dogs and children are fearful of one another. Early socialization with children will help to prevent unnecessary aggravation between these two living beings, as will a sensitive preparation for the introduction of your dog to your baby. Make the effort and your dog will grow to accept and like children who in turn will enjoy your dog. (See photograph 24). There is no nicer sight than a child and dog enjoying each other's company. You will then realize it was worth all the effort.

CHAPTER · 9

Dogs and Children's Other Pets

WE used to have a quiet and rather shy black cat called Elgar. In fact, she was the first pet that I had been responsible for and she was well established in my home when Nimrod came on the scene. Their first meeting was uneventful. She kept a wide berth around Nimrod and he did a quick wee on the carpet, and that was it. There was never any confrontation. They just learnt to co-exist. Together they destroyed a chair. Elgar scratched and Nimrod pulled at the stuffing, and together they allowed mice to overrun the house in which we were living. A mouse literally scampered across the floor whilst our cat and dog dozed in front of the fire. Perhaps they mistook it for a clockwork one which was silent.

Nimrod accepted Daisy without any problems at all. As she matured, she became more dominant towards him. One look from her and he was out of his basket or off the sofa to make way for her; and he was twice her size. He never questioned her dominance over him. Neither did we.

Wally's introduction to Daisy was much more eventful. Daisy is a dominant dog, not with us, but with other dogs that come to our house, she is top dog.

We brought Wally home as a tiny 8-week-old puppy. The children had put out a few toys and chews for him (they bought them out of their own pocket money!). Daisy was nearly 9 years old and had never been interested in chews, not even as a puppy. The following incident happened within half an hour of our tiny furry bundle's arrival, after Wally had been in the garden and after he had had a little wander around. It all took place within half a minute. Daisy was lying in the hall with one of the chews, meant for Wally, just in front of her paws. Matthew, one of my children, was kneeling at right angles to Daisy and Wally was approaching from the front. As Daisy stared hard at Wally, I could see what was going to happen. I quickly told Matthew to put his hands behind his back as Wally ignored Daisy's warning stare and continued to approach. Daisy raised her lips and he still continued to make his way towards the chew. In a second, Daisy gave a warning growl and snap and although Wally had not been touched, he ran screaming up the hall. Yes, I was upset and worried if a third dog was such a good idea, but I knew what I should do: I ignored the whole incident. I did not tell Daisy off, just gave her a cursory stroke and left Wally. Within five minutes, Wally was wandering around as though nothing had happened. He had however, learnt an important lesson. Daisy is top dog and what she has she keeps (from him, not us) if she so wishes.

There were two further incidents, very similar in content during the next month or so and that was it. Daisy and Wally play together sometimes and curl up on the sofa together when he is not in his crate; but Wally is under no illusion as to where he is in the canine hierarchy. He is at the bottom and secure in the knowledge of his position.

Many people worry about introducing dogs and other animals to one another. It is often presumed that all sorts of problems will arise. Whilst some dogs are undoubtedly easier and more accepting of different life forms around them, and others may become nervous or simply overexcited, most dogs and other animals can live side by side if a little thought is given to the situation.

Cats

With a cat that is already resident in the household, there are some preparations that should be made to make life easier for the cat when an inquisitive puppy is brought into the family home:

1. Put the cat's litter tray and feeding bowl on a surface the puppy cannot reach. This should be done well ahead so that the cat can get used to using his new area.
2. Allow the cat a comfortable area to which he can go to escape the attentions of an excitable puppy.
3. Cat flaps are very popular, but if it is large enough for a puppy to go through and particularly if it leads to a street or unfenced garden, you will have to accustom the cat to using a door or preferably a window, to come in and out of.

Introductions

Puppy to Resident Cat
The first meeting is all important. A puppy should not be allowed to

bound up to a cat in an uncontrolled way, nor should the children 'force' them to meet and make friends. Kneel on the floor and restrain the puppy by holding him in your arms and allow the cat, if she so wishes to come and investigate the new arrival. Then feed the cat her favourite food and put the puppy down.

Many cats keep well away from a new arrival initially. They may sulk or arch their backs and hiss; but once the newcomer's behaviour becomes more predictable, the cat should return to normal. Chasing of the cat should never be encouraged and the two animals should not be left alone unsupervised until they have developed an accepting relationship. Playing with the puppy while the cat is around will help to distract the puppy and help him avoid trying to play with an unwilling playmate of a different species.

Kitten to Resident Dog
The rules for introducing a new kitten to an established dog are similar to above, the most important being to give the kitten an escape route and never to allow any chasing.

Caged Animals

These include rabbits, guinea pigs, hamsters and other similar pets. These are unlikely to cause problems. They spend much of their time in the cages and if taken out, it is best to ensure the dog is not in the same room, unless he is on a lead to start with and controlled by someone other than the person with the other pet. If a rabbit is allowed in an enclosed run in the garden, the dog should be on a lead to start with, until his behaviour is acceptable and predictable. The dog should be prevented from tormenting the rabbit. The dog should also be prevented from running at the cage or intimidating the occupants by staring for hours.

Introducing a Puppy to a Dog that is Established in the House

Dogs are not like humans. We are brought up to be compassionate to the 'underdog'. Dogs have no such compassion. No fairness. To them they are either above another living being in the hierarchy of life, or below them. It is us humans that lead a more complicated existence.

When there is more than one dog in a household, there is a very definite pecking order between these canines. The humans have to be the 'ultimate' pack leader, but within the canine group there will be a leader and follower(s). The leader, as we know, has all the privileges; he eats first; goes through doors first; has the most safe and comfortable place to rest or sleep; wins all tug-of-war games over a toy; has first greeting and prime access to his pack leader; in this instance that is the humans. Our dogs are dogs and they instinctively understand all this. They become confused if we try to treat them like humans, where we for example give a lot of attention to a visitor who comes to stay, offering them the most comfortable chair and serving their meal first, urging them to start before it gets cold.

When a young puppy is introduced into a household with an established dog, he will already understand all about hierarchies, there having been a dominance hierarchy within his litter of which he will have formed an integral part. What is confusing for dogs and may upset what might otherwise be a simple existence are our values of fairness and compassion. The humans have to support the top dog. His position *vis-à-vis* the other dog/puppy, needs to be seen by him to be accepted by his pack leaders, all of you. The underdog will not resent this; he will not think it unfair; he will accept the pecking order contentedly, no questions asked.

The rules for the introductions are as follows:

1. **Discipline:** if the older dog disciplines the puppy over toys, access to resting places or play that is too rough, this should not be interfered with. The older dog would become confused and may feel the need

to prove his position more forcefully, and interference by the owners would wrongfully make the puppy feel that aggressive games are accepted by the owner.

If your old dog is very accepting, placid and patient in temperament and allows the puppy to play aggressively with him, the puppy will learn that is the way to play with other dogs; and when he becomes more mature and is running free in the park, this kind of playing will not be acceptable to most other dogs now that he is no longer a puppy and may, therefore, be viewed as a threat. To prevent this occurring, you should allow the older dog to discipline the puppy if he plays too roughly and that means when he uses his teeth excessively. If the puppy continues, then you should discipline the puppy.

2. **Children:** the children have to be helped to see that the puppy must not get more attention than the older dog. This can be difficult, particularly for younger children, but it is essential. Explain why and monitor the situation carefully. The children, if old enough and sensible enough, could play with the dogs individually; this will help the older dog feel his position in the household is the same, and will help the puppy relate to the humans.

3. **Time on his own:** your puppy should be separated from the older dog during his unsupervised moments. That is when you are out and when you are asleep. This is not because the older dog may savage the puppy (this is extremely rare). It is in order that the puppy relates to all of you more than the other dog. If most or all the play and comfort for the puppy comes from the older dog, that is who he will relate to. When he is older, all he will want is the company of other dogs. He should play with you more than the other dog. We all love to see a new puppy curl up with an older dog, but the puppy is to live in a human society and must relate more to them than to canines.

4. **Change in the hierarchy:** when a puppy is brought into a house with an older dog, the older dog will feel himself to be more dominant. This may change once the puppy reaches maturity and it can be difficult for owners to allow an old favourite to be dominated by a seemingly young upstart. Allow this changeover and support the new top dog and you should not experience any problems.

Adopt a positive approach with the introduction of the animals to one another. Be sensible and try not to let the dog see that you are in any way worried or expecting trouble. A matter of fact attitude is best.

CHAPTER · 10

Unsociable Behaviour

I THOUGHT I had prepared for everything when we decided to have a third dog. Wally was to be crate trained which I felt would cut out most of the accidents with chewing and housetraining which can occur even in the most vigilant of households. I lead a very busy life and I knew that crate training provides essential support. There were, however, two weeks in June when life was even more hectic than usual. I was on Jury Service, the children were on holiday and we therefore had a kindly soul to look after them and the dogs while I deliberated upon other people's problems. When I returned to the fold in the evenings, chaos was an understatement as I walked the dogs and fed the family.

One day during this period of 'happy families', my husband came home to find a parcel for him. It was a specially bound edition of a brilliant musical performance, in excellent condition and very rare; and in the kitchen I was given an excited talk on the qualities of the delightful parcel. I then continued my housewifely duties and he put it upstairs on the bed.

When things had settled, I went down to my office to do some work. Suddenly, Thomas came down and said that Wally had chewed a bit of the specially bound edition of my husband's new record. Well, my heart jumped out of its cavity. I rushed upstairs (husband was in the living room, listening to the gramophone) and viewed the evidence of the disaster. Thomas magnanimously asked if I wanted him to tell Daddy and I, feeling that it would be a bit unfair for him to experience too closely what I knew was to come, thanked him and suggested he went to bed. I put Wally in his crate to prevent further problems (a bit like closing the stable door after the horse has bolted, I know . . . !) and crept downstairs to await an almighty explosion. Well, I thought my time had come. My husband is normally so quiet and placid, but he became like a volcano at the beginning of a particularly violent eruption. I simply did not know what to say. 'Sorry' seemed so totally inadequate.

Fortunately, at my husband's place of work, there are a wonderful breed of people called restorers and they were given the task of putting together Wally's little moment of folly. Poor husband; at the office, they all found it highly amusing, having a wife who is supposed to be able to prevent just such mishaps, with a new puppy who should never have been in a position to cause such disaster. And it was preventable. That is the frustrating part of the whole business. I wanted to throttle Wally; however, to give him a telling off after the event might have made me feel better, but it would have completely confused him.

Everyone experiences problems with their puppy at some stage of the puppy's life, even in the most conscientious of households. How you handle a problem as it appears can make the difference between perpetuating it or nipping it in the bud so that it is a 'one off'. Prevention is always easier than cure with all problems, but even the best laid plans can come to grief in a few easily unguarded moments.

Who is the Boss?

Although not all dogs are dominant, it can be normal behaviour for a dog. A dominant dog may be male or female and will be a rather pushy individual who often makes sure he is the centre of attention. He demands to be petted and played with, tug-of-war being his favourite game, and will not make his grooming session easy by standing there. He may bite the brush, or your hands and may sit, lie, or roll over to prevent you continuing. Passively dominant dogs (those who have shown no sign of aggression), are usually very friendly and are often described as overfriendly.

Prevention

Pack Instinct
Your dog may not look anything like a wolf, but he still has some of the same basic instincts as his ancestors. One of these is pack instinct and the most important element in this instinct is that there has to be a leader. It is perfectly natural for a dog to assume this role for himself if leadership is not forthcoming from those around him. Do not be fooled – even the smallest Yorkshire Terrier may take on this role given half a chance. But, fortunately for us, dogs can just as easily assume a subordinate role; that is one of the reasons they have lived and worked with us for so long.

Dogs must be subordinate to humans – *all humans* – from the gruffest grandpa to the most adorable gurgling baby. The dog must be at the bottom of the pile, so to speak. He must be more important than the plants, but less important than everyone else. Of course we all love our dogs and they are an important part of our lives, but, they must never feel they are the most important. Your dog is an animal; he should not be treated like a human child, as that is not what he is. He is a dog and will be more content if he is treated as such. Dogs are far happier, more settled and more secure if they know their place within your pack. *Hitting him into submission will not make him feel subordinate. It will make him feel fearful and may well make him aggressive.* He is best made to feel subordinate in ways that he can understand. What follows is what would happen if he was in a wild pack consisting of dogs only.

1. **Feeding:** in packs in the wild, the dominant member will eat first. This is so the leader survives, he must get the most nutritious food, therefore he has the first pick of the kill – the others eat what is left. This occurs in litters of puppies. The next time you see a litter, observe how one pup will always grab the best teats (between its mum's hind legs) and he will not give way to another pup. Similarly, when pups are weaned, one pup will make sure he has the best access to food and may put his two front paws in the food dish to secure his position. This is natural behaviour. Therefore, bearing in mind that your dog regards you as the pack he belongs to and that he must be subordinate, he must be fed after you and your family. Prepare his food at the same time as you prepare your food. Put his to one side, eat yours, clear away, give him his food. Should you have a puppy on several meals a day, try to connect his main meals with yours. The important part is that he learns he has to wait for you to finish first.

2. **Sleeping:** in the wild, the pack leader will sleep in the safest, warmest, most comfortable 'den'. Often higher than the rest of the pack – if the terrain allows it. The subordinates will not sleep cuddled up to their leader, but further away on the fringe. Again, it is a question of survival. It is his responsibility to protect the pack and ward off intruders – generally he is responsible for his pack. You are the pack leader and not the dog, therefore he must sleep as far from you as possible, the kitchen or hall being the most usual place.

3. **Furniture:** if he is allowed on furniture, you should always be able to get him off whenever you want, as no place 'belongs' to him! All furniture belongs to his pack leader and he will understand that. This also includes his basket, you should be able to remove him

from it and sit in it yourself – leaning on it will suffice if you have a Chihuahua! If he is very dominant, he must not be allowed on the furniture as he should always be below your level.

4. **Tug-of-war and rough and tumble games**: all dogs play games and they are all played for a reason, not purely for recreational purposes. Tug-of-war is a game of possession. Dogs play this game to see who is the most dominant. (A naturally submissive dog will probably not play this game at all.) The most dominant one is the one who keeps the article. What usually happens in this game is that tug-of-war is played for a while – then the human gets fed up and lets go – leaving the dog to go off with the prize which he then believes he has won. This enhances his status. You should win the games by retaining the article. Under no circumstances should there be any growling.

   Rough and tumble should never be played at all. The dog will always have a sensation of winning.

5. **Attention**: the pack leader demands and gets. That is his right. If a subordinate dog demands attention from the pack leader and the leader is not feeling like giving attention, he would give the subordinate a lip curl or a growl.

   How often does your dog nudge you for attention? Or drop toys on your lap wanting play? Or worse still bark until he gets what he wants? Rather too often? Well he shouldn't, so ignore him. He must earn his privileges. Make him do something for what he wants; for example sit, lie down and so on. The attention he gets should be on your terms and not his.

6. **Grooming**: wolves groom each other in the wild. When the bitch (pack leader) grooms her pups (subordinates) they fully accept it. They certainly would not bite her nose! Your dog should not mouth or bite your hands or the brush; he should at least just stand there – if not actually enjoy it. He should be groomed every day (even short-haired dogs) to teach him that you are the boss and can handle him as and when you like, not when he chooses.

7. **Doors and stairs**: the pack leader goes first; it is his privilege and his responsibility to see what is ahead. You are the pack leader – or should be – therefore you go through doorways and narrow openings first. If your dog is lying in your pathway, make him move – do not step over him. In the wild, subordinates will always make way for the pack leader. Similarly, your dog should not be allowed to rush upstairs and stare down at you as you walk towards him. He is not the king of the castle.

Your dog has the capacity to be a wonderful companion. He deserves the best. To him the best is not to be treated as a human buddy but to be treated like the lovely dog that he is.

Cure

The cure for passively dominant dogs (dogs that have not bitten) is the same as prevention, but for an older dog it is better if you make one change to his life each week, allowing him to get used to that change before going on to the next.

Start with the change you feel will be easiest for him, gradually progressing to more difficult changes. For example, changing his feeding to after your meal may be easier than getting him out of the bedroom (see page 88, Sleeping Arrangements).

Attention is a very important part of the change to his life. He must learn that it is not his right to demand attention and get it whenever he wants. You should play with him whenever *you* want, not when he demands it. Making him do something for what he gets, to sit or lie down for example, will help him to realize that he has to earn his privileges; and making him go through doors after you will help him realize that he is not important enough to go first.

If your dog has shown any aggression to you or anyone else, you should go to your veterinary surgeon and ask for further advice. He may refer you to a behaviour counsellor to help you with your dog's problems. Your dog may have already taken a step up the dominance ladder and will require more special help; or his aggression may be due to an entirely different cause.

If you are not experiencing any problems with your dog, there is no need to make changes to his life.

Chewing

Prevention

Between 4 and 6 months, the puppy loses his milk teeth and his adult teeth start to come through. The puppy feels the need to chew during this stage and this need to chew may continue for another few months as the teeth settle into their jaws. Pulling wallpaper off the walls or scratching up the carpet is not chewing (see separation anxiety, page 102). Chewing the children's school shoes or the table leg is! (although this may also be caused by him becoming anxious when you are out).

1. Prevention is easier than cure; therefore you must keep tidy. Very young children are often just as happy playing in a play pen

surrounded by their toys. This will prevent many toys being quickly demolished by a playful puppy.

2. Do not give the puppy some of your old discarded shoes or slippers (or anything else) to chew. He cannot tell the difference between old and new; one shoe is much the same as another to him.

3. When you cannot watch him, either put him in his crate (see page 36) or a playpen. There are some specially made for puppies; a good pet shop might help you to find one, or fix a fireguard (the special type for use when children are in the house) around his basket. He should become accustomed to being on his own, from a very young age (see page 33) for short periods.

4. Provide him with items he can exercise his need to chew on, such as hide chews and nylon bones. Pet shops usually have a good selection.

5. If he picks up anything he shouldn't, he should be *immediately* stopped with 'NO' or 'Aaah!' If possible, from the puppy's point of view, the punishment is best seen to be coming from what he is picking up. If every time you picked up certain objects you received a shock in the form of noise, loud enough to make you jump, you wouldn't do it very often. Puppies are no different in that respect. The noise should be loud enough to make him jump. Clapping a couple of pan lids together can work well, but you must do it as he is picking up the object. If you make the noise as he is running off with his 'find', he will think it is OK to pick things up, but just not to run off with it.

6. Telling him off after the event is useless. He will have no idea what he is being told off for, even if you take him to the chewed object and show it to him. If you tell him off when you come home for chewing in your absence, for instance, if you do it often enough, he will begin to associate your home coming with a telling off; *he will have no idea it is because he has chewed*. To him a telling off will be because there is a mess around and because you have come home. Soon, these two things together will make him feel anxious and he will expect a telling off as your key goes into the lock. He is not 'looking guilty' because he has chewed.

7. Puppies (and dogs) are clever little creatures. They will continue to do things if it gives them pleasure. That pleasure can be in the form of attention from you. If, therefore, he picks up something he shouldn't and gets a game of chase (catch me if you can), although he might lose the article in the end, the chase will have given him sufficient reward within the first few seconds of him having picked up the object, for him to try again. Puppies and dogs who do this are

easy to spot. They will usually pick something up and dance about in front of you, or find some other way of making sure you notice. Shock as in No. 5 will prevent this behaviour.

Cure

For puppies, following the advice given above will stop destructiveness fairly quickly.

For older dogs with a really ingrained habit of chewing, the cure requires more effort and it is important to assess why he is still chewing:

1. Boredom.
2. Separation anxiety.

Boredom

Dogs that are bored will usually start chewing after their owners have been out for a while. It is only when he has been on his own for a length of time, that the dog becomes bored and starts looking for destructive entertainment.

1. Before you go, take him for a really good walk (off lead – running in a safe exercise area) and make the walk interesting for him by perhaps encouraging him to find things (see page 74, Hunting), so that he is mentally as well as physically tired.
2. Leave a bone for the dog which he only has when you are out. If it is left lying around all the time, it is not special.
3. If you are going to be out all day, coming back at lunchtime and taking him out for a walk (or asking someone to do this for you) may help.
4. This type of problem can be dealt with by punishment/shock which is seen to be coming directly from what he is doing. Double sided sticky tape on furniture works well for some dogs, as does a smearing of English Mustard or horseradish. Booby traps may also be employed, so that when the dog is doing something he shouldn't, he is instantly deterred, by, for example, a number of tin cans with stones in (top taped over) cascading on top of him as he pulls a tea towel from the radiator.
5. Crate training (see page 36) is also a solution, but not if you are going to be out all day.

Separation Anxiety

Dogs that are anxious about being left on their own perform a variety of behaviours to try and deal with their anxiety; they may bark or whine, urinate and/or defecate, but by far the most use destructiveness as an outlet. This can take the form of actual chewing or scratching at the door, or walls surrounding the door, or tearing up the carpet or linoleum, again particularly around the door frame. *He is not exhibiting this behaviour out of spite*; he is anxious about being left. Punishment will only serve to heighten his anxiety as it is usually given long after the chewing has taken place and he will have no idea why he is being punished.

The treatment for all is the same; the dog must get used to being confidently on his own. These dogs are usually overattached to their owners, following them around the house unable to remain in a room by themselves. They are often very affectionate. Buying another dog to 'keep them company' is not the answer; you may well end up with two dogs with the same problem. It is a common misconception that if you come back at lunchtime, the dog will become less anxious. In fact he will become anxious twice instead of once.

Your Relationship with Your Dog

Your dog needs to become more independent from you, in order that he can learn to accept your absence from the house. You need to become less the centre of your dog's life and your relationship with him needs to be cooled. Ignore his demands more; do not constantly give in to him. Generally, you should interact less. Do not feel so guilty about leaving him that you try to compensate for your absence by being over-affectionate and attentive to make up for it. The difference between you being there and not being there must be less marked.

Sleeping Area

Having your dog in the bedroom at night and keeping him in the kitchen, for instance when you go out, often causes severe destruction. Gradually getting him out of the bedroom (see page 88, Sleeping Arrangements) and settled in another room, downstairs, will help him to detach himself from you. However, some dogs will immediately stop chewing if allowed access to the bedroom during their owner's absence. There is inevitably an element of risk that you will have to take with this, in that he might chew in the bedroom; but he may settle quite happily, being in the area that he is most familiar with, that smells most of you. If you want to try this, start with a short time of 15 minutes or less.

Protection for Your Dog
If he tends to chew wires or other objects of potential danger to him, you need to consider excluding your dog from these items until you are able to complete the practical training below.

Muzzles can offer good, emergency protection for a short time, maximum of 4 hours only. Buy a basket type enclosed muzzle, as it is possible to feed him titbits with it on, making his acceptance of it easier. Firstly, let him familiarize himself with it. Then put it on leaving it unfastened and *immediately* give him a titbit. Take it off when he has finished it and whilst he is still relaxed. Gradually increase the length of time it is left on, always making sure he associates it with pleasure. When he accepts that stage, put it on and fasten it up, again giving titbits. This is not a long term solution.

Garages and porches can offer emergency protection, as can crate training, but he must get used to the crate first (see page 36, Crate Training).

General Tips To Help Reduce Your Dog's Anxiety
1. Punishment applied after the event will not tell the dog why he is being punished.
2. Sometimes close the door when you make a cup of tea, so that the dog does not always follow you around.
3. For many dogs, a good period of exercise off the lead, and then a meal, produces a desire to sleep. Exercising him before you go may increase the likelihood of success.
4. Ignore your dog for about half an hour before you go out.
5. If you tend to have the radio on when you are in, then leave it on when you go out.

Housetraining

Prevention of accidents
See page 34.

Cure
Puppies around 15 to 18 weeks of age or over which are persistently relieving themselves in the house have a problem.

1. Crate training, as in Chapter 4, once you have got him used to it, will produce a very good result in a short time and with a really persistent problem, this is the best method. He should go in this whenever you cannot watch him. The rules are that he is either in his

crate or being watched, or in the garden where you can keep an eye on him to see if he goes or not. Otherwise, he could just go into the garden, sniff around a bit and come back and mess in the house.

2. If he messes regularly on one particular spot, thoroughly clean that area using a biological cleaner, and feed him there; leaving the bowl there often produces good results.

3. Clean all spots he has 'gone' on very thoroughly with a cleaner specially made for the purpose obtainable from veterinary clinics or pet shops.

4. If you do not have room for a crate, he can and should be confined in some other way, perhaps using a fireguard, for short periods when you are unable to watch him, such as when you are cooking a meal or bathing the children.

5. If the housetraining problem is very sudden in onset, take him to the veterinary surgeon; he may well have an infection.

6. A male dog may start to cock his leg on reaching 9 to 10 months old or later in the larger breeds. What he is doing is marking his territory. It is a problem when done in your house but it may be acutely embarrassing when done in someone else's house. You may need to become more dominant with him generally. Castration can be very successful in dealing with this type of problem.

7. Submissive urination: some young dogs pass a few drops of urine when greeting people. This is a submissive gesture *and in no way is he to be punished*. These young dogs usually grow out of this behaviour, but in the meantime kneel down and greet him in a way that appears less overpowering to him or ignore him altogether until he is calmer, when you should stroke him calmly.

Jumping Up

This can be viewed as sweet in a puppy but is definitely not sweet in an adult dog with muddy paws that might land on your shoulders. (See photograph 21). It may be a sign of dominant behaviour.

Prevention
To prevent jumping up you should consider the following:

1. Always bend down to the puppy when he comes to greet you.

2. He should never be stroked unless he has all four paws on the ground.

3. Any attempt to jump up *instantly* stops the strokes he receives from you. Continue when all four paws are on the ground.

4. If you have an excitable puppy, greet him calmly.

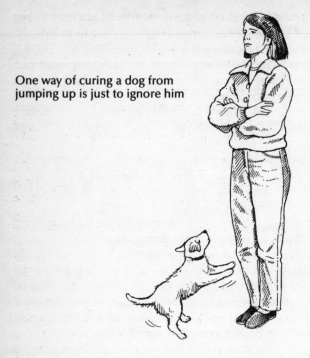

One way of curing a dog from
jumping up is just to ignore him

Cure

There are several methods and one will suit your dog. You may need to
try more than one method to see which one produces the best results.
Do not hit him with a rolled up newspaper. This may well overexcite
many dogs and make them fearful.

1. Ignoring takes longest but it works extremely well, because jumping
   up is a way of getting your attention. Ignoring means pretending
   your dog is not there. It means walking straight past him and when
   his four paws are on the ground, he gets a calm stroke, as in No. 3
   under Prevention above.
2. As he jumps up, get hold of both his front paws and hold them close
   together, but only hard enough to prevent him getting down when
   he wants; the object is not to hurt him. Continue to hold, until he is
   really struggling. Do not say anything to him. Let go when he is
   desperately struggling to get down and stroke him calmly when all
   four paws are on the ground. Repeat immediately if he jumps up
   again. This method will require a few repetitions. If you are standing
   there holding his paws and he appears to enjoy the experience, this
   method is not for him!

3. A dog cannot sit and jump up at the same time! Therefore, telling him to sit and then giving him a stroke will stop this behaviour. However, it will only work if your dog is not too dominant, because telling him to sit is still giving him the attention he is demanding by jumping up.

4. If your dog jumps up without bouncing about too much, it may be possible to put one of your feet on one of his back paws and press lightly at first, increasing the pressure until he moves his foot and has to get down. Again, the object is not to hurt him, just to make him uncomfortable.

5. Children and visitors: it is very difficult for visitors to use any of the above methods unless you know them well, (for young children it is not possible at all, apart from perhaps number 3). When you have guests, adults or children, put your dog on the lead and put your foot on it, making it tight enough for him not to be able to jump up but long enough for him to be able to stand. (See photograph 22). like this, you can give your full attention to the visitors and not to the dog. Ignore him and neither you nor the visitors are to speak to him or stroke him until he has calmed down, whereupon he can get a quiet stroke.

People who know the dog well, such as extended family members, are often the worst culprits, as they often say, 'Oh, it doesn't matter, he is such a lovely dog'. It does matter and your dog will not realize that he can jump up at some people and not at others. Consistency is what the dog understands.

Mouthing/Nipping

Many dogs use their teeth on almost anything. This activity may seem harmless and playful in a puppy (even though his teeth are needle sharp!), but if it is not stopped it will develop into bites when he is older. It may seem playful, but it must be stopped.

Prevention

Mouthing or nipping is difficult to prevent, but not entering into games that seem to overexcite him will help to keep this activity to a minimum.

Cure

Hitting him on the nose either with your hand or a rolled-up newspaper usually makes puppies snap back *and should never be done*.

For a puppy under 16 weeks a quick, immediate shake by the scruff of the neck, as you growl at him in a really gruff voice, staring at him and not letting go until he has averted his gaze is usually sufficient to control mouthing or nipping. For some puppies, giving a loud, sharp squeal (enough to startle him) and quickly withdrawing your hand as if you have been really hurt, can also stop this behaviour.

For puppies over 16 weeks, this may make him more 'mouthy' and determined and he may be becoming dominant so you will need to put into action the plan to make him more subordinate. Putting a taste deterrent on your hand may help during the process, as may giving him a quick squirt on the nose with ice cold water.

Thunderstorms and Guy Fawkes

Many puppies and dogs are naturally frightened of bangs and loud noises and may cower in a corner. Guy Fawkes comes round once a year and thunderstorms are not a constant feature of life. Therefore, your dog will come to no harm if you just let him crawl into a corner. Trying to comfort him will seem like praise and will only serve to perpetuate this behaviour. This can seem a harsh attitude as we are brought up to be compassionate and comforting to those who feel troubled, but dogs are not humans. Ignore him and he will bounce back as soon as it is over as if nothing has taken place. If he becomes excessively distressed and does not relax soon, when all is over, consult your veterinary surgeon for further advice.

Recall

Dogs often do not come back for a variety of reasons; they may have been chastised for not coming back quick enough, or they may be having more fun than they get from their owners.

Prevention
See Recall Training on pages 56 and 68.

Cure
Review recall training bearing in mind that if he is not coming back for food, he is not hungry enough. Feed him when you come back from the walk rather than before. In addition, you can re-train him to come back to a whistle.

1. Buy a whistle and at each of his meals, as you put his food down you give one or two blasts on the whistle. This is the only time you use the whistle for 2 to 3 weeks. You are getting him to associate the whistle with food.
2. After 2 to 3 weeks, still using it with his meals as above, try it when he is not doing much in the house, unconnected with his meals but

immediately he comes he is given a tasty titbit. If he comes running, you know you are progressing.

3. After a few days, when you are confident that he will always come in the house, whatever he is doing, try in the garden, as you did in the house, still using the whistle with his meals as in No. 1 above.
4. When he is coming well in the garden, still use the whistle with his meals, but now take him to the park and when he is not too distracted and you feel he will probably come anyway, use the whistle and give him a really tasty titbit as he gets to you.
5. Gradually increase the distractions and continue to use the whistle with his meals until he is coming well in the park.

Barking

Although it is natural for dogs to bark at something that alarms them, dogs which bark incessantly cause intense irritation to a very large number of people.

Prevention

This is very easy with a puppy. Simply *never* reward barking in any way. Remember, if there is nothing in it for him, he will stop doing it. Puppies will often start to bark in excitement and this can be unwittingly encouraged by the owner responding to the dog, either by directly praising or by giving the puppy what he has barked for. It may be a toy or attention, or to be let in or out, for example.

1. Completely ignore the barking and insist on at least ½ to 1 minute of quiet before you let him in or out. If he is barking for attention, completely ignore it; you give him attention when you want, not when he demands it.
2. Do not shout at him to 'be quiet' or words to that effect! This may raise excitement levels and increase the barking.
3. *He should not be hit for this (or any other problem).*
4. If you feel he is barking out of fear, do not try to comfort him, this is seen as praise to a dog. Do not tell him off either. Ignore him.

Cure

To cure barking problems you should consider the following:

1. If the habit is not too ingrained, institute all four points above. It may take longer for an older dog than for a puppy, but it will work with patience.
2. A more habitual problem will require water. A quick squirt on the

dog's nose with ice cold water works well, but it must be done the second he starts. Command 'Quiet' in a normal voice and give a quick squirt.

3. Barking for attention may be due to dominance and in addition to ignoring the barking, you may also need to make him more subordinate.

The successful solution to many problems relies on the correct assessment of the dog's behaviour. If you have any difficulty, there is no need to feel you have to live with it for the rest of your dog's life. Most behaviour problems are relatively easy to solve.

Go to your veterinary surgeon in the first instance, he may be able to help you himself or he may refer you to one of a growing number of behaviour specialists who will be able to help you sort out the problem, therefore enabling you and your dog to live a more mutually satisfying life together.

CHAPTER · 11

Mummy, Where has Fido Gone?

NIMROD has given us wonderful fun and happiness. He has been a joy to have around, friendly to everyone, animals and humans alike and the times we have been annoyed with him have been few and far between. For all he has given us, he has asked for nothing in return.

Old age in a dog (as in humans) can bring with it many things. In Nimrod, it has brought Spondylitis (inflammation of the spine) which in turn has caused him to become incontinent of urine and faeces. Living with this is extremely difficult in a not too large family house where the dogs live inside with us, but we are learning to cope with it. Because of this Spondylitis, Nimrod requires help to get into the car, he cannot get upstairs anymore and he does not wag his tail, a curiously sad phenomenon. He is also virtually deaf. However, he still enjoys his twice daily walks in the woods, running, not so fast now, after things thrown for him and bringing them back for another go; sniffing to see who has been in the woods since his last walk or just bumbling around behind us. He requires rests on these walks now, whereas, at one time he would keep going for hours; and that is why we go the relatively short way to the woods by car, as he could not manage to walk to the woods (and back) and still have fun actually in them. He still eats well but he sleeps a lot.

We all know that he now has a short time left and it fills me with indescribable sadness. The children are old enough to have some understanding of death, but I feel that they, like my husband, are more concerned at the moment, on the effect his death will have on me.

A number of people have said to me that surely the time has come to 'have him put down'; 'how can we live with incontinence?' 'and he spends most of his time sleeping.' The most important being we have to consider is Nimrod. He is not in pain and he is not distressed by his condition; it is inconvenient to us. Nimrod still enjoys life. Yes, he sleeps a lot, but he enjoys his walks, his meals and just ambling around the house and garden. He is still able to give and receive pleasure.

The day will come, unfortunately sooner rather than later, when, unless he dies naturally, we will have to make the momentous decision as to whether his life is to continue or not. This is the most awesome decision to have to make and I am honestly dreading it. I do know however, that when the time comes, we will take it with Nimrod's best interests in mind, not ours. We owe it to him to look after him in his old age and I do it with pleasure (mostly), thinking of all the fun he has given me; and without him, this book would never have been written. When he can no longer enjoy his walks or his meals, when there is no quality to his life at all, or if he is in pain that we can no longer alleviate, I will then, with the help of my family and veterinary surgeon, decide his time has come to an end. Thinking about it is distressing enough. Coping with it will be far worse. The death of a dog, like the death of a human member of one's family, is a bereavement and needs to be treated as such.

Dogs die for a variety of reasons. They can die naturally of old age or illness, be killed in an accident, or are euthanased to enable them to die painlessly for reasons of ill health or some behavioural problems.

Euthanasia

This is decided upon with the help of your veterinary surgeon, when the dog has no hope of recovery from an illness or accident and is distressed or also in pain. The decision is made with the dog's best interests in mind. We all wish our dogs would, when the time comes, die naturally in their sleep; sadly this does not always happen. Dogs are given an overdose of anaesthetic directly into a vein and death follows immediately, sometimes before the injection is finished. It is quite painless and the dog appears, literally, to have ' gone to sleep'. Hence the term 'put to sleep'. In death, your dog may lose control of his excretory functions; this is quite normal, although many owners are embarrassed by this.

Euthanasia can be carried out either at the surgery or in your home. This is a decision between you and your veterinary surgeon. Although he is in the business of saving lives of animals, he will have euthanased dogs before and will be understanding of your grief. He will understand that some of his clients wish to say goodbye to their pet and hold him until he has gone, while some will wish to say goodbye and leave their pet in the veterinarian's hands, with the understanding that it is done immediately.

The Body

With humans, burial or cremation and all their preparations and the service that accompanies them, are all part of the mourning process. This is denied to us with the death of our companion animals. Disposing of the body in a fitting manner can help.

Garden Burial

If your garden is large, this may be the most satisfactory solution, if your dog has not died of an infectious disease. Indeed, most of the big estate mansions have their own pet cemetery. Planting a tree or other plant over the grave can be a lovely reminder of the life your dog gave to the family he was so much a part of. There are regulations regarding the burial of dogs – your local Environmental Health Department should be in a position to advise you.

Pet Cemetery

These cemeteries are the same as human cemeteries and your veterinary surgeon will be able to help you find the nearest one to you and they will help you make arrangements for your dog's burial.

Cremation

This service exists in most areas and again your veterinary surgeon should have the relevant information. You will, if you so desire, receive a casket with your dog's ashes to dispose of as you wish. Keeping it on the mantlepiece is a bit morbid, but burying it in the corner of a small garden and planting a shrub over it, or scattering his ashes on his favourite walk, may help the mourning process.

Communal Collection of Bodies

Bodies are collected communally in all parts of the country and your veterinary surgeon can arrange this. The bodies are placed in black sacks and put at the bottom of a tip.

The death of a dog is unfortunately an experience all dog owners have to go through. Their lives are sadly relatively short and unless the owners are very old themselves, the dog will die before they do.

There are many organizations to help people cope with the death of a human loved one, but the death of a dog is unfortunately regarded by many non-dog owners as a minor hiccup in an otherwise normal life. For the owner it can have a devastating effect, and lack of understanding by others may increase the bereaved owner's feelings of intense sadness or even guilt over their dog's death. Although it is accepted that there is a period of mourning around the death of a close human, mourning over the death of a dog is considered to be 'overdoing it'. However, mourning is a vital ingredient in being able to continue with life after death in a fulfilling and satisfactory way. Grief counsellors to help cope with the death of a pet are now available in some areas.

Children and the death of Your Dog

For children, this may be their first experience of death and mourning. How it is handled may affect their attitude to future bereavement within the family. Young children may not understand the meaning of death, but it is important, nevertheless to answer their question of 'where has he gone?' honestly. Telling them that their pet has gone for a long walk or gone to live elsewhere, perhaps with other dogs in the sky, may leave them forever hoping that they will see their pet again. This wish can never be satisfied.

Honesty will help them to understand your grief and that the grief and sadness accompanying death is an important part of being ultimately able to accept that the dog has died. Accidents and natural death following an illness are usually relatively easy to explain; euthanasia is not.

Chosen Words For Euthanasia

The terms you use are important with children of all ages. The normal, colloquial term 'put to sleep' may induce feelings of panic in some children, particularly at bedtime; will they wake up in the morning? If they have to go into hospital and need to be anaesthetized (put in a deep sleep so they do not feel anything) will they wake up afterwards?

It may perhaps be more helpful to say (if the children are old enough to understand), in your own words, that he has been given a special injection which only animals can be given, to help him die without pain or suffering; to help him die peacefully; because animals do not understand pain and suffering in the same way we do. Children need not be present when their pet is euthanased.

Mourning

Children (and adults) must be allowed to be upset, however the pet has died. They may need to miss a day or two from school. They should be allowed to talk about the good times they have had with their dog and how much they miss him. It may also help to talk about what it is you all miss particularly. In this way, death becomes part of life; trying to pretend it has not happened, to spare the pain of knowledge, is not only disrespectful to the companion they may have shared a large part of their life with, but will also not help these children to accept the natural feelings of sadness and loss that they might have. Bottled up feelings can become like a gnawing sore that may erupt in all kinds of inappropriate ways.

Children are very sensitive and can accept the truth of many difficult situations better than some awkward cover-up that they sense is not quite right. Sharing the pain of death of a much loved dog, will ease the sense of loss and enable the family, as a whole, to enjoy the memories of all the good times he gave you and perhaps when all is calm again, to grow forward to accepting another companion in their lives.

CHAPTER · 12

Golden Rules

1. Every dog should be a wanted one. Make sure you really want a dog before you get one and that you can cope with the ups and downs a dog will bring to your life. It must be a decision that all members of the family make and should never be a surprise present.

2. Dogs are easy to obtain but not all are easy to live with. Choosing the right type of dog for your circumstances will help to make your relationship together a satisfying one for both.

3. The background of the puppy and the circumstances he comes from are vital when choosing a dog with children in mind, particularly young children. Take time to choose carefully.

4. Start as you mean to go on. Decide on practicalities and attitudes that are to surround your dog's life, so that your dog grows up in an atmosphere of consistency.

5. Help your children to accept that the dog is a living being and not a toy. Teach them from the outset how to play with him and mutual respect and affection will grow between the dog and child from your efforts.

6. Training a dog should be fun for him and all of you. Dogs must learn to respond to everyone in the family, including children. Train him in a positive way and he will enjoy the interaction, and be willing to please.

7. You are responsible for your dog's health. He cannot tell you when he feels unwell, but by your daily observation, you will know when he is physically not as he should be. Take him to your veterinary

surgeon and he will help your dog to become fit and healthy once more.

8. Dogs and children need to be helped and taught to relate positively to one another. Making the effort to do this will lessen the likelihood of any aggressive incident.

9. There is no reason why dogs and other animals should not live happily, side by side. Carefully thought out introductions and a positive approach will help your dog live with the other pets in an acceptable way.

10. Prevention is always better than cure.

11. Accept your dog's death, and the loss it has brought to the family; mourn him. Then enjoy the memories and all the fun he gave you during his life.

12. Your dog has the capacity to be a true companion. Do not abuse the trust he puts in you. You owe it to him to make his life interesting and the effort you put in will be amply rewarded by his delight at pleasing you.

Enjoy your dog.

Appendix

Useful Addresses

The Association of Pet Behaviour Counsellors
257 Royal College Street, London NW1

Treating behaviour problems in cats and dogs takes time to establish cause, develop treatment plans and offer practical advice to owners. The APBC is a nationwide network of experienced professional behaviour counsellors, available exclusively on referral from veterinary surgeons, to offer that time and expertise at affordable cost. Fees may be recoverable in part or full under many pet insurance policies. The APBC believes that behaviour problems in pets can be treated kindly through understanding and detailed personal consultation with the owner.

The Kennel Club
1 Clarges Street, London W1Y 8AB

The Kennel Club has names of registered breeders. There is also a junior section which provides encouragement for junior handlers.

The Blue Cross
The Editor, Pawprint Magazine, Blue Cross Field Centre,
Shilton Road, Burford, Oxon OX8 4PF

This is a rescue organization for a variety of animals, including dogs. *Pawprint* is a magazine for young owners, published three times a year. Further information can be obtained from the above address.

Pro Dogs
Rocky Bank, 4 New Road, Ditton,
Maidstone, Kent ME20 6AD

This is an organization which promotes responsible dog ownership.